"Four fabulous Grammies have done everything possible to make your life as a grand-mother easy, simple, and most of all, FUN! Just as you wouldn't travel the world without a map, you shouldn't embark on a journey to Grammie-Life without The Grammie Guide. *Where was this when I needed help with my first grand?...This book satisfies every need and every question. Treat yourself!"*

—SHARON LOVEJOY, author/illustrator of *Toad Cottages & Shooting Stars: Grand-ma's Bag of Tricks—130 Wonder-filled Activities* and *Roots, Shoots, Buckets & Boots*

*"*The Grammie Guide, *based on both time-honored wisdom and recent research, is a widely inclusive guide to making the most of time with young grandchildren. A first time gram-mie will find great guidance here, and those with experience will find new sources of in-spiration. It goes to the heart of what grammies can provide—one of the most special of relationships."*

—JUDITH A. MURPHY, M.D., Stanford University-trained pediatrician

*"*The Grammie Guide *will increase your awareness, playfulness and resourcefulness. While you don't need a book to love your grandchildren, this one will definitely enrich the time you spend together!"*

—RAHIMA BALDWIN DANCY, early childhood educator and author of *You Are Your Child's First Teacher*

"Historically speaking, grandparenthood—as a typical stage in life—is brand new. It's no wonder there are few social norms guiding "right" and "wrong" ways to grandparent. Yet, more families are including grandparents and great-grandparents than ever before in hu-man history; and let there be no doubt, multigenerational families may be (and should be) the best thing that ever happened to children. The Grammie Guide *helps to set the stage for guidance about being the best grandparent ever. Read it and become a part of this unprec-edented movement in the service of children."*

—LAURA L. CARSTENSEN, PH.D., Fairleigh S. Dickinson Jr. Professor in Public Policy, Professor of Psychology, and Director, Stanford Center on Longevity

"Reading all of these wonderful ideas makes me look forward to being a great-grandmother someday."

—BETTY PECK, ED.D., author and revered kindergarten teacher for over 50 years

"The Grammie Guide *gets back to the basics. Many children these days are absorbed by too much screen time. It's through the strengthening of imagination and role-playing that they develop a positive sense of self. This book gives grandmothers the know-how to form strong bonds with their grandkids through imaginative play. Truly a great tool based on sound child development research."*

—JOHN PINA, PH.D., child and family psychologist

"Grandparents, look no further for just about anything having to do with your grandchildren. It's all here. Parents, aunts, uncles and care givers, this is for you too—stock full of helpful, clever and practical projects and ideas. Four grandmothers have joined forces to share their expert advice and create a helpful, clever and practical guide to grand parenting."

—VALERIE V. LEWIS, nationally known author, expert on children's literature and founder of highly acclaimed Hicklebee's Bookstore in California

"There is something soothingly authentic about grandmother wisdom that touches and reassures the heart that all will be well. How lucky we are to have a volume of inspiration for simple pleasures to nurture these treasured relationships between generations. Not only have the authors gathered tried-and-true ideas from their role as grandmothers, but also in their professional roles as educators of young children.»

—ANNA RAINVILLE, M.A., Waldorf teacher, mentor, author and Ambassador for the Decade of Childhood

"Your young grandchildren will thrive with the bright, inspiring and easy-to-follow guidance of The Grammie Guide, *an amazing and helpful book of activities and advice to suit the needs of a child in today's busy world. I especially recommend the guide's approach to creativity and exploratory quality art in the chapter, 'Your Grandchild, the Artist.' Your young grans will have so much fun exploring their inner Picasso, van Gogh, Dali and Pollock. I'm delighted to highly recommend* The Grammie Guide *and plan to use my copy with my own grandchildren one day as we sculpt, glue, collage, paint, draw and celebrate memorable holidays through art."*

—MARYANN F. KOHL, author of more than 20 award winning art books for children, www.brightring.com

"Where was this book when I was a new grandmother? It would have become my bible for grandparenting...a MUST for every new grandparent and a wonderful entertaining and helpful resource for those of us who have been at it for over 20 years!"

—KATHARINE A. PERKO, former Arizona County Superintendent of Schools and Grandmother of 10

The
Grammie
GUIDE

Book design by Katie Jennings
Printed and bound in the United States of America.

Published by Tell-A-Gram Publishing, LLC in the United States.
1173 Shasta Avenue, San Jose, California 95126.
www.thegrammieguide.com

ISBN 978-1-4675-4486-3

ACKNOWLEDGMENTS

Like raising a child, writing and publishing a book is both challenging and rewarding. We gratefully acknowledge those who supported us throughout the process: Ellen E.M. Roberts for her expertise and fresh perspective as we developed the raw manuscript into the book you see today; Katie Jennings for her inspired design and cheerful readiness to make yet another tweak; our families and friends whose enthusiasm for the book sustained us; and finally our husbands. Little did any of us know how long this project would take. Bruce, Dave, Dick and Jim, thank you for your patience and encouragement. We know there were times when you wondered if this book would be finished before we all became **great grandparents!**

WE LOVINGLY DEDICATE THIS BOOK
first to our children who made us grandmothers
and then, of course, to our precious grandchildren:
Elizabeth, Caroline, Casey, Luke, Noah, Ryan, Ellie, Annie,
Carter, Connor, Riley, Tyler, Ellis, Cami, Tanner, Jackson,
Cassidy, Sawyer, Reagan, Brock, Shea, and J.J.
You have been and continue to be our inspiration.

The Grammie GUIDE

ACTIVITIES and ANSWERS for GRANDPARENTING TODAY

Jan Eby

Laurie Mobilio

Lynne Noel

Cindy Summers

TABLE OF CONTENTS

A Note to Our Readers

We four friends, two of us early childhood educators, became grandmothers within a few years of each other. Just as we had shared so much as mothers, we now began sharing our experiences as grandmothers. Best of all was our exchange of ideas for fun activities with our newest family members…games to play, songs to sing, books to read and places to go with our young grandchildren. Time passed and we continued collecting ideas, often being asked by other friends such questions as: What book or toy would a three-year-old like? What were the words to that marching song? How do you make playdough?

The Grammie Guide began with a box of index cards and our scribbled notes about favorite lullabies, books, toys and simple art projects. It grew over time into the book you hold in your hands today. Twenty-two grandchildren later, we now share with you what we have learned, hoping to make your grandparenting days as joyful as ours have been. We have done the research on child development for you, tested all the activities and offer practical advice on what equipment you need. And, there's a special chapter for Grandpa as well as one on staying connected with grandchildren who live far away.

The world has changed since we raised our own children. Though today's technology serves adults well, it has turned child's play upside down. Hours that once were spent exercising imaginations, minds and bodies may unfortunately today be spent passively in front of a screen. Here is where you, Grammie, can make a significant difference in your grandchild's life.

With face-to-face fun and developmentally healthy ways to spend time together, you can offer a slower pace in today's hurry-up world. *The Grammie Guide's* pages are packed with low-tech, easy to engineer, indoor and outdoor activities that will arm you with wonder-filled, yet simple ways to play, create and explore together. We've even sprinkled the book with our own lessons learned.

A child's days from birth to kindergarten fly by. *The Grammie Guide* will help you make the most of this special time. Just pick and choose what fits you and your grandchild best and, with confidence, let the fun begin!

Introduction

by Linda Lear

If I had influence with the good fairy who is supposed to preside over the christening of all children I should ask that her gift to each child in the world be a sense of wonder so indestructible that it would last throughout life...

—Rachel Carson, *The Sense of Wonder, (1956).*

The four experienced and sublimely resourceful grandmother-authors of *The Grammie Guide* have given us a wonder-filled book of possibilities for companionship with our grandchildren—whether they live across the street or across the country. Their suggestions provide unfailing antidotes to the boredom and disenchantment that come with the sterile preoccupation with things that are artificial and alienate both child and adult from the sources of their strength.

From the seeming passivity of the infant, the multisensory needs of the toddler, to the exploding cognitive demands of the preschooler, *The Grammie Guide* encourages us to re-discover the creative potential of the ordinary. Here are no suggestions for expensive toys or fancy vacations. We need nothing but our own imaginations to make everyday activities a source of shared discovery and companionship. The back yard, the driveway, the mail box, the grocery store, the park, the garden, a rainy day, a pile of leaves, a pail of water and a paint brush are all the ingredients necessary for imaginative play and for sharing something wonderful together.

Rachel Carson believed that if a child is to keep his inborn sense of wonder, with or without fairies, he "needs the companionship of at least one adult" with whom to share it and to rediscover with him the joy, excitement and mystery of the world we live in. *The Grammie Guide* allows no sense of inadequacy for any Grammie, new or old to the role of grand parenting. The authors understand that it is not as important to tell as it is to show, to appreciate, and especially to share. Here is a guide for producing indelible and irreplaceable memories. Here is also a guide for being that good fairy of childhood and for creating and nurturing a lifelong "sense of wonder."

Linda Lear is the author of *Rachel Carson: Witness for Nature* and *Beatrix Potter: A Life in Nature.*

CHAPTER 1

GEARING UP FOR GRANDCHILDREN

WELCOME, GRAMMIE! YOU HAVE JOINED THE RAPIDLY GROWING RANKS of America's 70 million grandparents, a full one-third of the U.S. population. Every day nearly 2,500 women in the U.S. become new grandmothers. Each will find her own unique way to interact with and express her love for her grandchildren…and so will you.

A BIT OF BACKGROUND: GRANDMOTHERING THEN AND NOW

The grammie born over a century ago was fully incorporated into the lives of her grandchildren, often living as part of the extended family under the same roof. She was part of a Norman Rockwell world where she cooked and gardened and stayed engaged with her children and grandchildren all her life.

There is no typical grandmother today—grammies fill many more life roles in our complex society than they did in the one Rockwell illustrated.

FAMILIES ARE FAR MORE DISPERSED DUE TO INCREASED MOBILITY AND JOB AND LIFESTYLE CHOICES. As a result grandmothers seldom live in the same home as their grandchildren or even in the same town.

MORE WOMEN WORK OUTSIDE THE HOME THESE DAYS. A grandmother may be employed herself or need to provide care for her grandchildren because their mother has a full-time job.

THE VERY STRUCTURE OF FAMILIES HAS CHANGED. There are traditional families, single parent families and blended families. Consequently, there may be only one or there may be several grandmothers in a child's life.

WITH THE FOCUS ON YOUTH AND THE EFFECT OF HEALTHIER LIFESTYLES, PEOPLE NOW LIVE LONGER AND ARE PRODUCTIVE INTO LATER YEARS. A grammie, then, may choose to continue working or have the luxury of pursuing her own interests—volunteer work, hobbies or travel, for example.

Despite all these changes, a grandmother's love for her grandchild and her desire to be part of his life remain the same. Likewise, a grandchild's need for the unconditional love of a grandmother is as true today as it has been for generations.

VISITING BACK AND FORTH

FAMILIES FIND WAYS TO BE TOGETHER REGARDLESS OF THE DISTANCE BETWEEN THEIR HOMES. A grandmother's urge to satisfy her need for a "grammie fix" and see her grandchildren is often the impetus to plan visits back and forth.

The first visit with your grandchild

WHEN AN INFANT IS BORN, IT IS MOST COMMON FOR GRANDPARENTS TO VISIT AT HIS HOME. As you may recall from your own experience as a mother, new parents tend to be protective, especially of their firstborn. Respect this and follow their lead as you are introduced to your grandchild. Also, there may be differences in parenting styles between you and your children, so when you visit, offer advice only when asked. Instead, bring along your patience, your acceptance and your sense of humor.

IF YOU WILL BE STAYING FOR A WHILE, PACK AS YOU WOULD FOR ANY TRIP. Take along your medications, as well as copies of your prescriptions and your doctors' phone numbers. For air travel, pack gifts in the suitcases you will check. If you want to carry them on the plane with you, leave them unwrapped to avoid hassles at security.

BE SURE YOU ARE WELL RESTED BEFORE YOUR TRIP. The arrival of a new baby is exciting but demanding. You may be called on to help out in the home—cooking, cleaning or laundering. Taking care of these household chores can be a blessing for the overtired parents of a newborn. If there is an older sibling, you can help by keeping him happily occupied. When your children know that you are there to love and keep their children safe, you are giving the most valuable kind of support.

> *Jan:* When my twin grandchildren were infants, I managed the visits of friends by setting aside one afternoon as an Open House. I invited friends and neighbors to stop by for lemonade and a short visit to get a peek at the new babies.

CHILDPROOFING YOUR HOME

IS YOUR HOUSE GRANDCHILD-FRIENDLY? The age of your grandchild will help determine what you need to do to prepare your home. Naturally, an infant in arms requires different preparation from that for a busy, active toddler or preschooler. However, the following guidelines and comments apply to any young child.

Begin by using your common sense. Valuables or knickknacks should be placed out of reach so your grandchild will not be attracted to them.

LOCATE POSSIBLE DANGER SPOTS BY LOOKING AT YOUR HOME FROM A CHILD'S PERSPECTIVE. Get down on your hands and knees. What do you see that could be enticing to a crawling baby or curious toddler? Dangling drapery cords, lost coins under the couch, or your purse with all its potentially harmful contents (pills, nail files and sharp pens, for instance) can pose a risk to little ones.

Today there is more safety awareness regarding children than when we were raising our own families. As a result, there are many inexpensive products now available to pad sharp corners on coffee tables or hearths, secure cabinets and doors and shield electrical outlets. Consider these precautions.

Safety Checklist:

• COVER UNUSED ELECTRICAL OUTLETS with the small plastic shields sold at hardware or home improvement stores.

• LIMIT ACCESS TO UNSAFE AREAS with plastic door knob covers that require adult strength to open doors and use cabinet latches to keep cupboards locked.

• MOVE ALL CLEANING SUPPLIES from underneath sinks to higher locations or install child safety locks as described above.

• INVEST IN GATES TO PREVENT FALLS if you have stairs. Spring-loaded gates are fine for the bottom of stairways but it is strongly recommended that only the sturdier, hardware-mounted gates be used at the top.

• BE SURE YOU HAVE A WAY TO OPEN INTERIOR DOORS because a small child can accidentally lock herself in. Some locked doors can be opened by inserting a simple screwdriver in the keyhole; others need a specific tool. Know what you need and keep it handy.

Jan: Grandpa loves telling our grandkids the story of how he got locked in an upstairs bathroom as a young boy and required a rescue by firemen through the window. This is great family lore but not something we'll repeat in this generation because we know how to get those doors open.

• TAKE TIME TO INTRODUCE PETS to your grandchild. Even the most gentle dog or cat can nip or scratch when pinched or pulled by a young child.

• CLOSE EXIT DOORS SECURELY so that your grandchild cannot let herself out when your back is turned.

- **LOCK DOORS TO BALCONIES.** Children are tempted to lean over the railing to see what is below.

- **PUT HOUSEPLANTS OUT OF REACH;** many are poisonous.

- **REMOVE TABLECLOTHS** that a grandchild could grab. With a single accidental yank, even a small child can upset table lamps or risk injury from falling items.

- **SUPERVISE A CHILD'S TIME IN THE KITCHEN** as many cooking tools and all stoves are dangerous.

- **SECURE ALL WINDOWSCREENS** so that open windows are made more safe for children to watch what is going on outside.

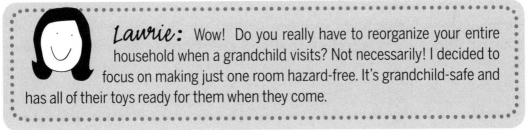

Laurie: Wow! Do you really have to reorganize your entire household when a grandchild visits? Not necessarily! I decided to focus on making just one room hazard-free. It's grandchild-safe and has all of their toys ready for them when they come.

Since it is not possible to completely childproof your property, be aware of where your grandchild is at all times, just as you did when your children were small. Hazardous areas that require constant supervision are:

- The garage with its tools, machines and chemicals

- Swimming pools, spas, fish ponds, bathtubs and any body of water even a few inches in depth

- The driveway because drivers may not see small children when backing up

- The garden shed, with its sharp tools and poisonous yard supplies

Even with preparation, there can be unwelcome surprises. Your son or daughter can tell you what things particularly captivate your grandchild. We know a three-year-old who likes to twist every dial in sight and a four-year-old who shows a fascination for matches. As our own grandmothers wisely said, "An ounce of prevention is worth a pound of cure!"

CHECKING PARENT PREFERENCES

One of the most important steps before you are left in charge is to ask Mom and Dad about how they want you to help care for their child. They may have very specific ideas of how to hold, feed and put their child to bed, and you will want to respect their wishes. For example, find out:

• What is the "going-to-sleep" routine?

• Is there a particular soothing technique the child likes?

• What is the usual eating schedule? What does he eat, how much and when?

• Does he take naps? When?

• What about snacks—any favorites or restrictions?

Once you talk about these things together, you will all feel more secure. Young parents will appreciate that you are trying to do what they do at home. And the more closely you follow your grandchild's familiar schedule, the sooner he will settle in.

 TIP: When you discuss routines with your children, write everything down. This not only helps you remember, it is good insurance when grandchildren try to convince you that Mom lets them eat ten cookies at a time!

GATHERING EMERGENCY INFORMATION

IN AN EMERGENCY, A QUICK RESPONSE IS CRITICAL. Here is a list of information you should have even when your grandchild comes for a short visit. Be sure it is handy so you or Grandpa can locate it easily. Keep a copy in your car, too.

- Phone numbers to reach Mom and Dad

- Child's doctor's name, phone number and address

- The name and phone number of a trusted pediatrician in your area if your grandchild is from out of town. Ask your own physician for a recommendation or check with friends.

- Letter giving you permission to make emergency medical decisions such as the sample Emergency Authorization Form in the Appendix.

- A list of each grandchild's allergies (food, medicine or insect)

- Poison Control Center phone number (1-800-222-1222)

- Directions to the nearest hospital or emergency center

- First Aid Kit and First Aid Book (one with large print and simple illustrations)

- Always remember 9-1-1. Children three and older can learn to dial this in emergencies.

Cindy: For many years I have been diligent about taking CPR courses because my husband has heart problems. When my first grandchild arrived, my daughter suggested that now I include CPR for infants and small children because the techniques are very different. Now I can help both adults and children in distress.

Documents for travel

INCREASED MOBILITY HAS MADE TRAVELING WITH GRANDCHILDREN—BY PLANE, TRAIN, CAR OR BOAT—MORE COMMONPLACE. Families plan reunions and vacations together and sometimes grandparents, rather than parents, escort young children. Be aware that rules today are far more stringent than they were before September 11, 2001. Check with your travel agent or online to be sure that you have all the documents you need (www.travel.state.gov). Know that travel to Mexico and Canada, once a breeze, now requires passports and powers of attorney to accompany a child just as for a trip abroad.

A WORD ABOUT TOYS

WAIT UNTIL YOU GO TOY SHOPPING FOR YOUR FIRST GRANDCHILD! The toy industry has changed radically in the years since we raised our own children. Although the old favorites are still available, it is hard to find them among the plastic, glitzy competition. Who are all of these strange fantasy characters, and whatever happened to Winnie the Pooh? Children and their parents are bombarded with talking teddy bears and dolls, movie and television characters, and electronic and battery-run everything!

Electronic and licensed character toys sell well and are initially attractive to children. These toys are widely advertised on television and seen in movies so children beg for them and have a preconceived notion of how to play with and use them. This leaves little to the child's imagination. He will probably tire of such a toy even before the battery runs out or be frustrated when he realizes that it does only one thing.

You can provide an entirely different world of play and activities for your grandchildren when they are with you. Be the one to offer toys that stretch their imaginations, build their problem-solving skills and empower them to direct their own play. What toys are these?

Open-ended toys

Our experience with our grandchildren, and in the preschools where we have taught, agrees with the research: children keep returning to toys that are "open-ended." These toys stimulate play in a variety of ways and foster a child's brain development by helping him integrate what he has learned or experienced in the past with new information. Blocks, puppets, balls and crayons are classic examples of toys with which children create their own plan for play, rather than simply pushing a button and watching the toy perform. The child, not the toy maker, determines what the toy can do. No electronic toy of any price can offer this to a child.

AS YOU WELL KNOW, GOOD TOYS ARE NOT ALWAYS THE MOST EXPENSIVE, and children do not need many. Look for those that are durable, well made and time-tested. Kids love trains and cars, cuddly dolls and stuffed animals, simple musical and rhythm instruments, small animal and people figures, art supplies and dress-up clothes.

Remember how many times your own children had more fun with the box the toy came in than the toy itself? Take advantage of that knowledge!

If you are lucky enough to snag large appliance cartons or packing boxes, they serve well as homes and hideouts for young homemakers or little pirates. In fact, lots of children prefer to play with things that are not sold as toys—plastic containers, yarn, paper tubes, old purses, scarves and jewelry for dress-up.

So, head for the toy store or neighborhood garage sale with these thoughts in mind. As you shop, you will be able to glide past the "plastic-fantastic" and reach the checkout counter with imaginative toys that span the ages... no batteries required.

CHAPTER 2

YOUR INFANT GRANDCHILD
(Newborn to 1-year-old)

NOW YOU'RE A GRAMMIE! HOLDING YOUR GRANDCHILD FOR THE FIRST TIME is an emotion-filled moment, whether you have waited for years to become a grandmother or it happened before you thought you were old enough. As you study his little face and admire those tiny fingers wrapped around yours, you marvel at this beautiful new life and the beginning of a new generation.

A GRAMMIE'S ROLE IN HEALTHY DEVELOPMENT

YEARS HAVE PASSED SINCE YOU HAD A BABY YOURSELF and perhaps you feel a bit awkward or have forgotten the techniques that were once so natural. Rest assured...like riding a bicycle, it will all come back to you. The mechanics of diaper changing and burping will again feel familiar and you will soon find that your soft voice, smiles, and unhurried, gentle care are all this little miracle really wants from you.

Respecting parental preferences

TODAY'S PARENTS HAVE THEIR OWN IDEAS of how a grammie fits into the picture when a new baby comes. It is best to remain flexible about what your role might be and let the new parents take the lead. They may have given you ultrasound snapshots of your grandchild in utero to show off around town and then invited you to the birth. On the other hand, they may hold you at bay until their nuclear family has bonded and it may be a few weeks before they invite you to visit. The new mom could be sent home from the hospital after a 24-hour stay and might welcome your help right away, or the new dad may take paternity leave and together they will manage on their own. Be patient, but be ready. Incidentally, paternal grammies may have to wait a bit longer; the new mom is more likely to ask for help first from her own mother.

ASK WHAT YOU CAN DO TO BE MOST HELPFUL. As you recall, newborns have many needs. The demands may seem overwhelming for first-time parents and that is why so many grandparents are asked to pitch in initially. Aren't you lucky? You have been there, done that and can be the extra pair of hands and the tour guide on this new adventure.

Cooking meals, holding Baby so Mom can take a shower, taking charge of a night-time feeding so parents can catch up on their sleep, entertaining siblings, running errands, keeping up with the laundry—the list of ways you can help goes on and on. Because fathers are so much more involved in childcare these days, supporting the new parents with non-infant chores will be welcome. It will be hard to resist reaching for that baby yourself, but your turn will come.

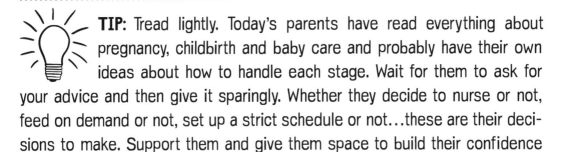

TIP: Tread lightly. Today's parents have read everything about pregnancy, childbirth and baby care and probably have their own ideas about how to handle each stage. Wait for them to ask for your advice and then give it sparingly. Whether they decide to nurse or not, feed on demand or not, set up a strict schedule or not...these are their decisions to make. Support them and give them space to build their confidence as parents.

Following Baby's routines

KNOW HOW HER DAY GOES BEFORE YOU TAKE CHARGE. Those first few months are times of flux as the baby and her parents settle into their new routine together. By the time she is three months old, your grandchild will probably have a schedule of feeding times, awake/asleep times and bath times. Stick to the routine when she is with you; it is better for her and her parents will appreciate it.

HOW INFANTS LEARN

A CHILD'S BRAIN IS LIKE A SPONGE. Every minute a baby is awake, he is taking in the world around him. Scientists now tell us that the younger the brain, the more malleable it is. It builds itself by forming connections in response to the stimulation it receives. From the moment of conception, the neurons, or nerve cells of the brain, multiply faster than any other cells in a baby's body. The rapid pace of brain development continues into early childhood: at birth, the brain weighs 25% of its adult weight; by age one, 50%; by age two, 75% and by age three, 90%.

As a baby is exposed to sights, sounds and smells, his brain continues wiring itself as a result of what he experiences. A baby's brain is designed for learning which happens faster and easier now than it ever will again. For him, learning is pure enjoyment. The majority of his waking hours should be engaged in unstructured, hands-on play. This is how he discovers the world around him. He needs time to explore, pick up objects and examine them. Encourage his curiosity...it is exactly what he needs.

Screen time for infants? No!

NOW IS NOT THE TIME TO INTRODUCE INFANTS TO TELEVISION. Keep the television turned off. Do not buy into the claims that videos for infants build IQ. Instead heed the recommendation given by the American Academy of Pediatrics (AAP) that children under two years of age should not spend any time watching a screen. This includes not only television, but also DVDs, computers and smart phones.

Further, the AAP firmly states that the first two years of life are especially important in the growth and development of a child's brain. What is going on in the brain of a young child as he blankly stares at television? Not much. Just watch his eyes glaze over when he is in front of one.

Children need human interaction as well as to be actively, not passively, engaged with their environment. Young viewers spending time in front of television in these language-learning years miss vital opportunities to develop thinking and communication skills. This cannot be stressed enough.

EQUIPMENT

Just the basics

SOME THINGS HAVE CHANGED. Remember the equipment you used when raising your own children: crib, high chair and playpen? There is endless paraphernalia available today and much of it has a new look. Some grandmothers choose to convert a whole room into a nursery and outfit it completely—from expensive new furniture to coordinated bedding; others will want to have just the necessities without the frills. It is up to you.

HERE IS A LIST OF SUGGESTIONS FOR THE BASICS YOU WILL NEED—all the practical stuff—when your infant grandchild comes to visit. You may want to include items from the nice-to-haves list as well. Do not feel you need to buy everything new: try neighborhood garage sales, internet sites or loans from friends. (The list assumes that Mom and Dad will bring Baby's special items, such as clothing, toothbrush, pacifier, foods and medications, if any.)

For sleeping:

- CRIB, BASSINETTE, OR PORTABLE CRIB/PLAYPEN Cribs with drop-down sides are no longer considered safe. In fact, by law, they cannot be manufactured, sold or even re-sold at yard sales or online.

Here is a list of guidelines to evaluate whether a crib meets current standards. For a more detailed list and updates, check with the Consumer Product Safety Commission (CPSC) at www.cpsc.com.

- The mattress should be firm and fit tightly into the crib frame.

- There should be no missing or broken hardware or slats.

- Slats should be no more than 2 and 1/2 inches apart (about the width of a soda can).

- Corner posts or decorative knobs should not be higher than 1/16 inch above the end panels of the crib.

- There should be no design cutouts in the headboard or footboard.

- TWO FITTED CRIB SHEETS AND WATERPROOF MATTRESS COVER Pediatricians today recommend no pillow, blanket or bumper pads in the crib.

For diapering:

- A CHANGING STATION You can improvise by spreading a towel or a waterproof pad on a bed, a bathroom vanity or low chest of drawers. You can also set up a changing area directly on the floor, though it may be difficult to stand up from that position while lifting Baby.

• DIAPERS, BABY WIPES AND OINTMENTS Today diapers are sized according to an infant's weight. Parents can tell you the size needed and which baby wipes and ointments they use. With the recent focus on environmental issues, a controversy exists as to whether cloth or disposable diapers should be used. Follow the parents' preference.

• PLASTIC GROCERY BAGS These can be recycled for disposing of soiled diapers. Be sure bags are stored out of Baby's reach.

For bathing:

• BABY BATHTUB Choose one that is non-skid or use a bath seat designed especially for infants who can sit.

• BABY SOAP AND SHAMPOO These two products are often combined in body wash and are available in a variety of scents, some organic and hypo-allergenic.

• TOWELS   Use a soft, lightweight terry cloth towel or the hooded bath towels for infants.

• BATH TOYS FOR OLDER INFANTS Recent warnings recommend bath toys that dry thoroughly inside and out to prevent the growth of bacteria or mildew.

 TIP: Have all of the above items assembled before putting Baby in the tub. And do not forget the clean diaper and her next outfit!

For feeding:

If you are spoon-feeding the infant, it is done more easily when she is securely buckled in a reclining infant seat or, when older, a high chair. Check with Baby's parents about food preferences. Snacks, these days, can be anything from garbanzo beans to veggie crisps.

- BABY FOOD, CEREAL AND SNACKS

- SMALL SPOONS AND SIPPY CUPS

- BIBS

- BOTTLES AND NIPPLES

- FORMULA OR A SUPPLY OF BREAST MILK

 TIP: Those cloth diapers we used for our children are hard to find but make fantastic burp cloths—so much more absorbent than the ones sold for that purpose. To make great shower gifts, decorate the old-style diapers by stitching ribbon around the edge or down the seams.

For traveling:

- CAR SEAT It must meet legal requirements and fit correctly in your car. Need help with installation? Ask the baby's parents or check with your local police station for instruction. Car seats must be installed in the back seat and need to face backward until children reach the height and weight limits for the seat. See www.aaa.com for the latest regulations from the American Automobile Association.

- STROLLER Choose one that collapses easily for storage and is lightweight.

- DIAPER BAG Any bag large enough to carry the essentials will work. Backpacks are popular today for their hands-free feature.

For playing:

• BLANKET Spread any large and washable blanket or towel on the floor for Baby's play area.

• ITEMS ON HAND Many items from your kitchen, such as small plastic containers and measuring spoons, can double as toys.

• SIMPLE TOYS Choose toys of various colors, textures and sounds. Be sure they are easy for Baby to hold.

....

Safety Reminder: Consider the size and safety of any object you offer Baby. If something is small enough to fit through a toilet paper tube, it is a choking hazard and not safe.

....

Nice-to-haves

These are the extras that make baby tending easier, especially for longer or frequent visits.

Laurie: Those baby monitors are great! You can set up the transmitter in the baby's room and the receiving end wherever you are. No need to run back and forth to check if he's still asleep. You'll hear when Baby first begins to stir and scoop him up before he gets too upset.

• ROCKING CHAIR OR GLIDER

• BABY SWING

• SOFT TOYS AND BOARD BOOKS

• CDS

• PROTECTIVE COVER FOR THE BATH TUB SPOUT

• FRONT-PACK BABY CARRIER OR BABY SLING

HOW AN INFANT GROWS:

A Refresher Course

A REVIEW CAN BE HELPFUL. Even though you have been through it all with your own children, the following charts will remind you what your grandchild might do today and what comes next. This refresher is merely a guideline.

Remember that each child grows and develops at his own pace and gives his own twist to every stage he passes through. Though not all children reach each stage at the same chronological age, each child will follow the phases in order. Temperament varies too, and becomes apparent at a very young age. Your grandchild may be very active or prefer to play quietly, may be determined or more flexible, outgoing or cautious. Naturally, we love them all, just the way they are.

YOUR 1-3 MONTH-OLD INFANT MAY...	REMINDERS AND TIPS
Lift his head occasionally but lack the strength to hold his head steady on his own.	Remember the football hold? This is a perfect way to support his neck and head when moving him.
Be startled by loud noises and sudden movement.	Whenever possible, provide a calm environment.
Gulp air when crying or feeding.	Rub his back with a firm hand to get those burps up...he will not break.
Notice brightly colored objects eight to twelve inches away.	Provide color in his surroundings: soft toys, clothes you wear, wall decor.
Rely on crying to express his needs.	Respond quickly...is he wet, hungry, cold, hot, tired or bored? Old fashioned swaddling, now called the burrito wrap, is still recommended for Baby's sense of security.
Discover his hands.	Offer him a rattle. It helps him connect what his eyes see with what his hands do.
Begin swiping at objects he observes.	Dangle soft toys safely above him for baby batting practice.
React to voices and even smile in response to another's smile.	Smile, smile, smile. Talk, talk, talk. In fact, we wish that today's disposable diapers would have "Talk to Me" printed on them as a reminder that infants need to hear your voice and have as much eye contact as possible.
Look away, whimper or close his eyes, signaling overstimulation.	Respect his need for quiet time. He may want to be alone or rocked gently.
Show increased strength and body control by arching his back and lifting his legs when on his stomach.	Give him floor time on a blanket with a variety of safe toys. This is his equivalent to your workout at the gym.

YOUR 4-6 MONTH-OLD INFANT MAY...	REMINDERS AND TIPS
Begin to roll over.	Be certain she is lying in a safe place.
Enjoy being propped in a sitting position.	Use an infant seat or stroller or prop her on your lap.
Sit without support.	For practice, take her hands and make a game of pulling her gently up to a sitting position.
Stiffen legs and stand when held upright.	Support her and let her stretch those legs.
Reach out and grasp objects.	Beware! Guard your necklace, earrings and glasses...anything in her hands will go into her mouth.
Bang toys to hear the noise.	If you do not like the racket, give her something soft and less noisy.
Cry or fuss when a desired object is taken away.	Distract with another toy or move her to a new spot.
Begin to recognize familiar faces and objects and be increasingly social, responding with coos and smiles.	Make frequent eye contact and talk with her...the more the better.
Start teething.	Help her cope with gum discomfort using teethers, chilled washcloths or by massaging her gums with your clean finger.
Babble with her own form of baby talk, often in several distinct syllables.	Carry on "conversations" with her...this is important to her language development.
Use her hands to grab for a toy and transfer it from hand to hand.	Surround her with brightly colored, safe toys. Make a game of giving and taking.

YOUR 7-9 MONTH-OLD INFANT MAY...	REMINDERS AND TIPS
Bounce when held in a standing position.	Seat him in an activity saucer to exercise those legs.
Stretch his arms out to those he recognizes, but act shy or seem afraid of strangers.	Give him time to warm up to new faces, even yours, especially if he is not used to seeing you wearing your reading glasses.
Shift suddenly from laughing to crying.	Pick him up and distract him with a toy or song.
Start to creep with his tummy still on the floor.	Be watchful. He can move faster than you think. Is the area safe?
Imitate the syllables and sounds he hears.	Join him in sounding out what he has heard. If raised in a bi-lingual household, he will practice sounds of multiple languages. Encourage him.
Understand that names, such as Mama and Dada, have specific meanings.	Use the name you want him to call you when you talk to him. "Grammie loves you" or "Come to Nana."
Be able to hold his own bottle with good hand to mouth coordination and drink at will.	Do not miss a chance to cuddle him, even when he is proudly feeding himself.
Bring hands together like a clap.	Begin a game of Pat-A-Cake.
Start to learn the meaning of "No" by the tone of voice used.	Create a space for play where there is less need for saying "No!"

YOUR 10-12 MONTH-OLD INFANT MAY...	REMINDERS AND TIPS
Crawl easily and go exploring with surprising speed.	Give her space but supervise closely.
Use touch and taste to learn about her environment.	Watch out! She will pick up and chew on whatever she finds on your floor.
Test the impact her behavior has on others. She seeks approval but, at the same time, may push boundaries.	Stay calm and be consistent in setting gentle limits. "Uh, uh, uh...be gentle with Fido's tail."
Pull herself to her feet and cruise around furniture.	Put her little feet in those non-skid socks that are sold today and pad sharp table corners for her protection.
Enjoy simple games like Wave Bye-Bye and Peek-A-Boo.	Capture these performances on your smart phone to use for Grammie brag time.
Feed herself finger food.	Know which foods can be offered to your grandchild. Cheerios are still a favorite or try the popular Goldfish crackers.
Cooperate in dressing.	Reinforce her efforts to help you dress her (raising her arms, sitting still). Thank goodness for Velcro, onesies, spandex and no-pin diapers...dressing infants is easier these days.
Express a wide range of emotions (affection, frustration, jealousy, humor).	Share books with mirrors and photos of infants as springboards for talking about feelings.
Respond to her name and say one or two words.	Be playful, repeating her words with her. Introduce other words to build on her vocabulary.
Understand many more words than she can verbalize.	Support her attempts to use baby sign language if her parents have introduced it. For more about this new, effective way to communicate with pre-verbal little ones, check online at www.babysignlanguage.com.

NEED SOOTHERS?

INFANTS CRY—IT IS A FACT. After making sure that all is well in the hunger and diaper categories, what can you do to calm a little one? It does not take long to learn what your infant grandchild prefers for entertainment and soothing. Today's bouncy seats, swings and portable cribs come with a variety of noises, songs and vibrations. Some infants like to sway, others to jiggle, and others just to be held. Your arms, voice and movement alone might do the trick.

As a refresher, here are some suggestions that work, with most infants, some of the time:

• USE THAT ROCKING CHAIR The rocking may put you both to sleep.

• HOLD BABY Move from side to side or gently bounce as you cuddle her. Pat or rub her back or bottom. Talk softly, hum or sing cheek to cheek.

Cindy: There is a special lullaby that I sang to each of my grandchildren from the time they were infants. I would hold them close and sing softly in their ear. Even before he could talk, my grandson would make the baby sign for "more" after I finished.

• VARY THE POSITIONS When one way of holding Baby does not work, another way might: tummy-down across your lap, cradled in your arms, or held upright looking forward or over your shoulder. When she finally falls asleep, the next challenge is to transfer her to bed without waking her— good luck!

• OFFER A PACIFIER If she is accustomed to it, a pacifier may soothe her. It has been given that name for a reason.

• WATCH A PENDULUM CLOCK The two of you together can follow the beat and sway with the movement.

• TRY A BABY SLING OR FRONT-PACK BABY CARRIER Close and secure, Baby is more likely to calm down.

• PLAY SOOTHING MUSIC There are some wonderful CDs available with soft instrumental music or sounds from nature that are calming.

• GO OUTDOORS Fresh air is good for both of you and a change of scene can distract her from what is bothering her.

• TAKE HER FOR A WALK in the stroller. Infants often settle down as you roll along.

• GO FOR A RIDE IN THE CAR Get her parent's permission. With her safely buckled into a properly installed car seat, the hum of the engine may put her to sleep before you leave the driveway.

• HAND BABY OVER TO GRANDPA Let him try to soothe her while you both keep your fingers crossed that Mom and Dad come back soon!

ACTIVITIES INFANTS ENJOY, ROOM BY ROOM

Fun in the kitchen

These days, parents may be too busy to linger and play in the kitchen with their baby. They have an agenda to fix dinner, clear the table or empty the dishwasher. You, as a grammie, can pause and introduce him to this special place, the heart of the household. Unlike a busy parent, you have time to chat face-to face with him about everything that is going on…this is how he learns.

An infant is so portable; he can join you almost anywhere. Seated safely in his infant seat or bouncer, your grandchild will be a happy camper as long as he can see you easily. From his vantage point, the kitchen is one of the most stimulating and interesting places to be with its constant activity, clanking pans and intriguing gadgets that move, buzz or beep.

What can you do here in the kitchen together? Ready, set, go!

• TALK AND SING AS YOU DO YOUR TASKS Infants love to hear you. Use familiar songs but change the words. For example, *Row, Row, Row Your Boat* can become something like, "Tap, tap, tap your spoon on your high chair tray, Grammie's oh so glad you're here. We'll have a happy day." Infants are a very forgiving audience so sing away!

• LET HIM SHAKE AND BANG Your measuring spoons in his hands turn the high chair tray into a noisy drum. Remember that everything goes into the mouth at this age so offer only objects that are too large to fit through a toilet paper tube.

Lynne: When one of our grandsons was about nine months old, he loved hearing me say "uh-oh" each time he dropped a toy on the floor from the high chair. To save my energy and my back, I attached his toys to the high chair with a chain of those colorful plastic links. We could still play the game but retrieval was much easier.

• TRY DISHTOWEL PEEK-A-BOO This is a classic game of surprise. Hide your own face first and, as your grandchild relaxes into the game, gently drape a towel over his face. After a few repetitions, he will giggle with anticipation when you reach for the towel.

> **Cindy:** I filled one low kitchen drawer with safe items for my grandson to play with and made sure other drawers and cupboards were latched. When he visited, he made a beeline, crawling toward his drawer of treasures, a sort of kitchen toy box. It was well worth having to reorganize the drawer when he was done.

• **WHEN HE CAN SIT ALONE ON THE FLOOR**   Surround your grandchild with colorful plastic containers or lightweight pots that he can hide things in, bang on or stack.

In the family room

• **GIVE HIM TUMMY TIME** Put him tummy-down on a blanket with a few toys. Today's infant who sleeps on his back will be more willing to try a new position for a while if you get down on the floor with him, too.

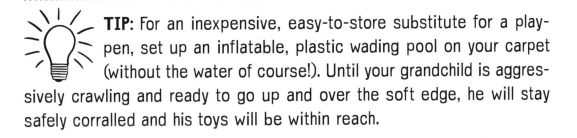

TIP: For an inexpensive, easy-to-store substitute for a playpen, set up an inflatable, plastic wading pool on your carpet (without the water of course!). Until your grandchild is aggressively crawling and ready to go up and over the soft edge, he will stay safely corralled and his toys will be within reach.

• **HOW BIG IS BABY?** With Baby facing you, gently take each hand in yours and touch them to his chest. Say, "How big is the baby?" and give the answer as you spread his arms high and wide, "Soooooo big!"

• **WHO IS THAT IN THE MIRROR?** With your grandchild in your arms, walk up close to a mirror. Smile at him and say, "There's Baby! And there's Grammie!" Take his hand and gently touch the faces in the mirror.

• **A ROOM WITH A VIEW** Put Baby in an infant seat in front of the sliding glass doors so he can see outside: talk about the flowers, trees, or the dog chasing his ball.

• MEET ROVER OR FLUFFY With Baby propped up or sitting next to the window and the family pet outside, the two can be introduced in a mutually safe and friendly way.

• RECORD HIS GROWTH A fun way to remember Baby's growth is to take a picture monthly with his age on a sign propped up nearby. It eliminates the question, "How old was he in this photo?"

• MONKEY SEE, MONKEY DO Babies love to imitate what they see adults doing. Give your grandchild a toy phone and he will hold it right up to his ear.

In the bedroom, hall or bath

• WASHING MACHINE ENTERTAINMENT If you have a front-loading washing machine, position the baby so he can watch the clothes tumble.

• TALK TO HIM As you fold clean clothes, make those socks into puppets or play Peek-A-Boo with Grandpa's tee shirt.

• HALLWAY EXERCISE A long hall becomes a perfect runway for new crawlers. Lure him with a ball or truck at the far end.

Lynne: My daughter-in-law had a great idea for protecting little fingers. She hung a washcloth over the top near the hinge of each inside door to keep it from closing. No pinched baby fingers in that house!

• BIG BED FUN What child does not like crawling around on a big bed? Pile up the pillows to plop in, snuggle together and pretend to sleep.

Jan: I put my plastic laundry basket in the bathtub so my granddaughter at seven months could sit in it with a few bath toys. She had the edges to hold on to and the toys were contained as the water flowed in and out. Of course I stayed right with her while she splashed.

GOING OUTDOORS

YOU DO NOT NEED TO HAVE A BACK YARD to enjoy the outdoors with an infant. A small area of lawn, a porch or deck, or a nearby park will do. No matter where you live, go outside with your grandchild and let the discovery begin. The warmth of the sun, the sound of raindrops splashing, and the tickle of a blade of grass are but a few of the outdoor treats that intrigue and fascinate even the very young.

 TIP: Remember that an infant's internal temperature control is not fully developed until the end of her first year. So for her to be comfortable, she should wear one more layer of clothing than you.

Try these outdoor ideas:

• GO FOR A WALK AROUND THE NEIGHBORHOOD to see what you can see. Infants are good observers. From the carriage or stroller an infant will stare with fascination at clouds moving across the sky, birds overhead or perhaps an airplane going by.

Cindy: While bragging to my dermatologist friend about how cute our new grandson was, she reminded me to be sure to protect his skin when I had him outdoors. For the first six months I kept him covered and he wore those darling safari hats and cool-looking baby sunglasses and we headed for the shade. Her advice for safe sun exposure after six months was to apply generous amounts of sunscreen made especially for infants.

• FEEL THE FRESH AIR AND GENTLE BREEZES Put the bouncer outside or spread a blanket on the ground or deck and enjoy the outdoors together.

• LISTEN FOR THE BIRDS Watch the tree branches sway and talk to her about what you see and hear. Maybe even sing about it.

• TOUR YOUR YARD Let your grandchild reach for, smell and touch the plants you know are safe.

....

Safety Reminder: Many common plants, such as oleander and poinsettia, are poisonous. Watch carefully. Everything goes into an infant's mouth.

....

• SET UP WATER PLAY If she can sit, put her next to a shallow container of water and watch her splash and plunk her toys. If the weather is warm, why not let her sit right in the container for an outdoor bath and play?

....

Safety Reminder: For any activity around water, constant supervision is required.

....

Lynne: Whenever I took my young grandchildren out, we took along a backpack we called the Go Bag. In it were extra diapers, wipes, bottle and formula, sun hat, change of clothes, the special blanket and anything essential for the day. There was still plenty of room to stick in my cell phone, wallet, emergency number, map...and we were ready to go!

• GO ON SIMPLE FIELD TRIPS Visit the grocery store, go window shopping or browse in a pet store. Try a trip to a petting zoo, an aquarium or children's museum. Some museums even have special exploration rooms designed just for infants. Keep a packet of wipes handy to clean those little hands.

Graduating to toddlerhood

Did it seem as if this year of your grandchild's life passed in an instant? Each time you have seen her, she has changed so much, and her repertoire of skills has exploded. Actually during these first twelve months she has grown and developed at a faster rate than she ever will again. That once helpless infant has graduated and is now a budding toddler.

CHAPTER 3

YOUR TODDLER GRANDCHILD
(1-year to 2 ½-years-old)

ON THE MOVE! TODDLERS ARE FEARLESS EXPLORERS...going where they have never gone before, fascinated with everything around them, awake more of the time, and displaying an increasing attention span.

THE BUSY TODDLER

CHANGES, ALTHOUGH EXCITING, BRING CHALLENGES, TOO. With newfound independence, your grandchild, now a toddler, is likely to become more assertive and at times more difficult to manage. Experts have noted parallels between toddler behavior and that of early adolescence, with its mood swings, testing of authority and wanting to be independent one minute and cuddled the next.

With toddlers our best advice is to gear up for the action. To encourage their active play and to relax and enjoy their company most, we suggest you arrange an area in your house where they have plenty of room. Toddlers do not sit still, stand still or even lie still. They do not wait around for things to happen; they make them happen. Are you ready?

A schedule can help

TODDLERS APPRECIATE PREDICTABILITY. Follow established patterns for mealtimes, naps, bedtimes and playtimes. When there is a plan for the day and you keep their normal routine, things are less apt to fall apart. Remember that a toddler can morph quickly from being impulsive and defiant one moment into a sweet angel the next. Some day you will both chuckle over the tales of his dramatic toddler tantrums.

A GRAMMIE'S ROLE IN HEALTHY DEVELOPMENT

EVERY WAKING MOMENT TODDLERS ARE LEARNING…from observing and listening to what is being said around them, to testing theories of how the world works, or watching and then mimicking how people behave. They repeat what they see and hear. If a toddler observes an adult frustrated in traffic, losing patience with a salesclerk or constantly eating junk food, she may understand those to be acceptable behaviors.

REMEMBER YOU ARE AN IMPORTANT MODEL. Share activities with your grandchild that are lively and positive. Be sure she sees you enjoying books, art, music and the great outdoors; and practicing healthy habits like exercising, eating nutritious foods and, of course, not smoking. As important, show her the pleasure you find in friendships, conversation and personal interaction.

Let your toddler set the pace while you play together

ALLOW HER TO DISCOVER ON HER OWN. While she plays, stopping often to concentrate on what she is doing, a toddler is using this unstructured playtime to integrate what she already knows with the new information she is gathering. Restrain yourself from hurrying her along or showing her the "right" way.

CHALLENGE TODDLERS' CREATIVITY WITH OPEN-ENDED TOYS. In addition to those toys she is accustomed to at your house, have a few others hidden away for when she needs a change. What is the favorite today...the red ball or the blocks?

Plan for active play

WATCHING IS NOT DOING. Toddlers love trucks and pull toys as they always have but in today's world there is competition for their attention as they are easily mesmerized by television and computer screens. We all know there will be a place and time for electronic entertainment but in the early years, active play remains the best way to enhance a child's physical and intellectual development.

The National Association for Sport and Physical Education says that toddlers should be actively engaged in self-directed play—play of their own choosing—most of their day. Offer your grandchild hands-on activities where he can solve problems, act out a story, take part with you in lively conversations and discover the world at his own pace.

Limit screen time

TOO MUCH TELEVISION MAY RESULT IN SHORT ATTENTION SPANS. Recent research supports this idea. A study by Dimitri Christakis, M.D. in the Journal of the American Academy of Pediatrics showed that frequent television viewers in early childhood were in the highest category of seven-year-olds to display concentration problems, impulsiveness and restlessness.

You know the addictive power of television and electronic games even for the very young. They may be used as a "babysitter" by busy parents and daycare providers but be sure that the time he spends with you is active and interactive.

 TIP: Remember that the AAP recommends no screen time for children under two and then a limit of two hours a day for older children including even quality television shows and videos.

Although there are no guaranteed ways to avoid attention disorders later on, promoting active play is a better use of your time together. It is the best way for children to learn. Hide that screen, pull the plug or just say you do not know how to use the remote.

Talk to your grandchild

LANGUAGE DEVELOPMENT TAKES A GIANT LEAP FORWARD AT THIS AGE. A toddler seems to understand everything you say. You will relish your conversations with your grandchild now because he is so responsive. By speaking slowly and clearly with him in the chatty give-and-take of playing together, you are providing a good language model.

And most important, show your interest

Your time and attention, one-on-one, tells a toddler he is valued. This sense of self-worth can contribute to his healthy long-term development. So grab his hand, get down on the floor and play away!

EQUIPMENT

Just the basics

LET PARENTS PROVIDE YOUR GRANDCHILD'S PERSONAL ITEMS: clothing, pacifier, special blanket, toothbrush, special foods and medications, if any. Meantime, here is what you will need for your toddler's visit. If you like, before you buy everything new, check out garage sales and internet sites or borrow from friends.

For sleeping:

- BED

For younger toddlers, a crib or portable playpen will do. Check with the CPSC to see that your crib meets current safety standards.

- No drop-down sides.

- The mattress should be firm and tight-fitting.

- There should be no missing or broken hardware or slats.

- Slats should be no more than 2 and ½ inches apart (about the width of a soda can).

- Corner posts or decorative knobs should not be higher than 1/16 inch above the end panels of the crib.

- There should be no design cutouts in the headboard or footboard.

For older toddlers who have learned how to climb out of a crib: a twin-sized bed with a guardrail, a futon or an inflatable mattress on the floor.

• **SHEETS,** waterproof mattress cover and blankets. Have extra sheets on hand in case of spills and accidents.

For diapering:

• **A TOWEL OR WATERPROOF PAD** Spread on the bed, either one makes a good changing area.

• **A FEW TOYS** Items, such as a small stuffed animal or book, can be used to distract her during the gymnastics of a diaper change.

 • **DISPOSABLE DIAPERS, BABY WIPES, OINTMENTS** Today's diapers are sized according to a toddler's weight. Check with parents for the correct diaper size and any preference for ointments. You will find baby wipes are almost indispensable and some come scented and pre-treated with salves.

• **PLASTIC GROCERY BAGS** These are useful for disposing of soiled diapers but should be stored out of the toddler's reach.

• **POTTY CHAIR OR SEAT** Check with his parents to see if he is using one at home.

Cindy: Distracting my two-year-old granddaughter, the wiggle worm, during diaper changes was challenging. When toys didn't work, I pulled out my bag of tricks. As with my own children, I sang silly songs to her or asked questions: "Where's your nose, your ears? Can you clap your hands?"

For bathing:

• BABY SOAP AND SHAMPOO These two products, some organic and hypo-allergenic, are often combined and are available in a variety of scents.

• TOWELS Toddlers love big, colorful towels.

• BATH TOYS We recommend bath toys that dry thoroughly inside and out to prevent growth of harmful mildew and bacteria. Small plastic cups work well for filling and dumping and rinsing soapy hair.

• NON-SLIP MAT To prevent tumbles, use a mat or bath seat attached by suction to the bottom of the tub.

• STEPSTOOL Hand washing, tooth brushing and admiring himself in the mirror are easier when he can reach the sink.

For feeding:

• HIGH CHAIR Choose a high chair or a portable booster chair equipped with a tray and safety straps. Look for the CPSC logo when purchasing a high chair to ensure it meets current safety standards.

• BIBS Eating is a learning experience for toddlers and can be messy.

Lynne: Pelican bibs are great for toddlers. They're the plastic ones with the trough that catches dropped food. My grandson knew that when a morsel in his hand missed his mouth, he could quickly retrieve it from his bib. It made eating much neater, and sure was cute to watch.

• PLATES AND BOWLS No need to buy special dishes, small plastic containers work well.

• TODDLER-SIZED SPOONS AND FORKS Some toddlers may still eat with their fingers.

• BOTTLES AND NIPPLES Infants and toddlers are weaned at different ages. Some toddlers still use bottles and will require several nipples for each visit.

• SIPPY CUPS These plastic cups with screw-on tops keep spills to a minimum.

....

OOPS! Toddlers' food often ends up on the floor. If you're worried about crumbs and spills, spread a beach towel or plastic cloth under the high chair. You'll be a lot more relaxed at meals and can clean up in a snap.

....

For traveling:

• CAR SEAT It must meet legal requirements and fit correctly in your car. Ask parents or your local police station for help with installation. Car seats must face backward until children reach two years or the maximum height and weight limits for the seat. See www.aaa.com for the latest regulations.

• STROLLER Select one that is lightweight and easily collapsible for storage and loading in the car.

• DIAPER BAG A backpack or large tote works well to keep the day's necessities all in one place.

For playing:

• COMMON KITCHEN ITEMS Small plastic containers with lids, pots and pans, wooden spoons and rubber spatulas are ready-to-use toys.

• SIMPLE TOYS A ball, some blocks, stuffed animals, dolls and cars/trucks are sure hits.

• BASIC ART SUPPLIES Toddlers are ready to use art supplies such as fat crayons, construction paper and sidewalk chalk.

- BOOKS Assemble a variety including board, cloth and other books with simple stories, lift-up flaps and photographs of children and animals. Choose from old familiar favorites that he can "read" on his own, new books to be savored together and ones that reflect his current interests.

Nice-to-haves

These are the extras that make child-tending easier, especially for longer or frequent visits.

- CHILD-SIZED TABLE AND CHAIRS These are handy for snack time, tea parties and artwork.

- A PLACE FOR HIS TOYS It can be a dedicated shelf, a box or a closet where your grandchild can consistently find his playthings.

- BATH TUB SPOUT COVER This decorative safety item helps your grandchild avoid bumping and touching the hot metal faucet.

- PLASTIC CLOTH OR BATH TOWEL These protect the floor during eating or art activities.

- MORE BOOKS You can never have too many.

 - TOYS Here are some proven winners for this age: push/pull toys, nesting toys, simple puzzles, rhythm instruments, a riding/scooting toy, dress-up clothes, a plastic tea set and an unbreakable mirror.

HOW A TODDLER GROWS:

A Refresher Course

NO TWO CHILDREN ARE ALIKE…as you know from raising your own children. Each child is different, but there is a progression all toddlers go through developmentally. We know that each child grows and learns at her own pace and according to her own interests and temperament. Though some things have changed in recent years for the very young, such as increased television viewing and enrollment in daycare, the developmental charts that follow still apply to today's toddler.

YOUR 13-18 MONTH-OLD TODDLER MAY...	REMINDERS AND TIPS
Use gestures to communicate.	Can she demonstrate how to say "Shh" or give you a high-five? She may also know baby sign language or just enjoy copying you.
Have trouble saying her name.	Be patient and practice with her. Girls generally develop verbally earlier than boys.
Like attention.	Describe what she is doing. "I see Sara holding her own cup," or "Look at you jumping, up and down."
Fear unfamiliar places.	Let her stand at the door a few minutes to size up what is going on before you both enter the room.
Be afraid of new people.	Let her stay at your side until she becomes comfortable.
Get frustrated when hands and feet do not do what she wants them to do.	Praise her efforts, coach her along and lend a hand if she will let you.
Cry if she does not get what she wants.	Ease frustration with kisses, kindness and cuddles, as well as by waiting out the storm.
Be attached to a favorite blanket or toy.	Treat the toy or blanket as a valuable object. Try to overlook its threadbare appearance.
Display possessiveness over toys she knows are hers.	Model sharing by handing her toys and asking her to give you one. "One for Grammie and one for you...may I have that one? We are sharing."
Be learning to follow instructions.	Make requests simple, such as "Please bring me your shoes," rather than "If you bring me your shoes, we can go for a walk."
Become picky about what she eats.	Do not worry...if she eats lightly at one meal, she will likely make up for it at the next.
Enjoy dumping and filling containers, turning knobs and pages.	Help her practice these developmental skills but supply appropriate props and set boundaries.
Climb and jump on furniture.	Designate chairs that are OK for climbing and beds that are OK for jumping. Stay close to her while she jumps.
Build towers of four or more blocks.	Show that a broader base will stabilize a higher tower. Boys are generally better at spatial perception than girls.
Carry the largest toy or the most playthings she can hold.	Encourage her big plans by providing large, lightweight toys.

YOUR 19-24 MONTH-OLD TODDLER MAY...	REMINDERS AND TIPS
Refuse to do what is asked.	Give short, simple directions and then follow through.
Push, pull, climb, drag and lift everything within reach.	Let him see what he can do as long as it is safe.
Move quickly from one activity to another.	Have lots of ideas for alternative activities in your back pocket; attention spans are short.
Be more interested in toys than playmates.	Remember, for him, playtime with peers is about the toys, not the interaction.
Resist getting dressed.	Dress him quickly while describing your next activity together.
Vacillate between newfound independence and babyish ways.	Support his independent attempts, but do not expect too much.
Begin fantasy play.	Encourage his imagination through simple playacting with dolls or stuffed animals.
Love to say "no."	Avoid yes or no questions. Instead of "Do you want to take a bath?" say "Now it is time to take your bath."
Throw screaming temper tantrums.	Rather than challenge him head-on, cajole, distract or let it run its course.
Walk up and down stairs.	Never let him out of your reach when he is on the stairs.
Begin to run and climb.	Provide a safe enclosed place and watch him.
Expand his vocabulary from 50 to 200 words in six short months.	Talk with him constantly while you play together. He will learn new words.
Repeat words overheard in conversation.	Watch your language and refrain from using baby talk because he will repeat what he hears.
Love repetition.	Teach him simple songs and poems.
Be able to wash his own hands.	Set a stepstool by the sink and be sure he can reach the soap dispenser. Stand by while he soaps up.
Help with simple chores like sweeping the floor and raking leaves.	Take advantage of this! You may never again have such a willing helper.

YOUR 25-30 MONTH-OLD TODDLER MAY...	REMINDERS AND TIPS
Give up afternoon naps.	Try sharing a book or story. A quiet time may be all she needs.
Have all her baby teeth.	Encourage tooth brushing.
Eat three meals a day plus one or two snacks.	Let her scrub a carrot or apple to interest her in fresh food.
Try feeding herself with a spoon.	Resist the temptation to feed her. She needs to practice on her own.
Cram food in her mouth and forget to chew well.	Never leave a child unattended while eating.
Talk to herself.	Respond to her chatter even if it is nonsensical. Ask her questions about what she is doing.
Walk longer distances.	Plan excursions in the neighborhood.
Jump off the bottom step.	Applaud her daring but be there to help if she needs it.
Balk at changes in routine.	Children like to know what to expect. Talk ahead of time about the activities you have planned.
String large beads.	Make a necklace for Mom.
Throw and kick a large ball.	Play ball with her...back and forth, back and forth.
Cry when parents leave.	Acknowledge the sadness and reassure her: "Mommy will be back after your nap." Then get her involved in an activity.
Turn pages of a book one at a time.	When reading together, ask her to be the official Page Turner.
Make demands and scream to get what she wants.	Wait it out. As a grandparent you are entitled to bribe, cuddle and comfort.

What about gender differences with toddlers?

Although gender differences are negligible until children are two-and-a-half, in general girls tend to talk and toilet train earlier, and boys develop skills like walking, lifting, kicking and throwing a ball sooner. Both boys and girls enjoy playing with balls, blocks and stuffed animals. Provide all types of toys for your grandchild...no matter the gender.

ACTIVITIES TODDLERS ENJOY, ROOM BY ROOM

Fun in the kitchen

The kitchen attracts children as it does adults and can be a great place for toddlers to play. First, however, make sure your kitchen is a safe zone for this age.

Safety Reminder: Electrical outlets capped? Appliance cords and pots on the stove out of reach? When cooking, use the burners at the back of the stove and be certain that handles on hot pans are turned to the side, out of reach of the toddler.

Now you're ready...watch for the smiles!

• DUMP AND FILL This is a favorite toddler game and the kitchen is a good place to play it. Give him a wide-mouth plastic container and he will soon discover that what goes in will also dump out, whether soft toys, mixing spoons or Cheerios.

• PLOPPING REAL FOOD Real food dropped into a pot is guaranteed to amuse most toddlers. Any sturdy piece of produce you have on hand is fair game. Offer oranges, lemons, carrots, small gourds or tiny pumpkins. Add a wooden spoon for stirring and pretending to taste.

• START A TODDLER BAND Encourage your toddler grandchild to compose rhythms by banging on your pots with large spoons or chopsticks. Two pot covers can be cymbals. Turn on some music and join the marching band yourself. Band members might even try plastic bowl hats on their heads to add to the silliness. Be sure Grandpa has his camera ready.

 • FEED TEDDY, TOO Teddy bear can join your grandchild at the table. Does Teddy need a bib? Your toddler will think it is such fun to help his friend "eat."

• **FINGER LICKING FUN** Mix up a batch of pudding. Wash your grand-child's hands, pop him in his high chair and scoop a spoonful onto the tray... it becomes an easel for his hands-on artwork.

• **SAVE YOUR EMPTY BOXES** Boxes from toothpaste, jewelry, checkbooks and cereal are all good sizes. Let your toddler grandchild experiment with stacking and unstacking them to build towers. He might even like to decorate some of the boxes with crayons or stickers.

Jan: Baskets and bowls make good beds for small dolls or stuffed animals. When my granddaughter was nearly two, I gave her doll a cuddle, covered her with a cloth napkin blanket and kissed her goodnight as I tucked her into our breadbasket. My granddaughter imitated this routine with her "baby," and repeated it over and over the way toddlers do. I still refer to it as the "bed" basket.

• **BUILD A TODDLER'S TENT** Drape a sheet over the kitchen table so that a young toddler can crawl in and out. How about playing Peek-A-Boo here? When a little older, your grandchild may take Teddy in with him and stay there to play. If you crawl in too, it is a great place to read a book together, hide from Grandpa or learn a new song.

OOPS! Watch your head when you crawl out and give the blood in your legs time to get back in circulation. Sitting cross-legged is a natural position only for toddlers and yoga gurus!

• **TODDLERS LOVE WORKING WITH PLAY DOUGH** Pretending to be a young chef, he will feel busy too as he squishes, rolls, cuts or pats, while you prepare lunch. Play dough can be purchased or made very inexpensively. See the Appendix for a recipe.

OOPS! Play dough "travels" in the hands of a young toddler. Keep him seated in his high chair or supervised at a play table until he is done. You will want to avoid the difficult chore of removing play dough from carpet or upholstery.

• **SET THE STAGE FOR TEA PARTIES** Dolls, stuffed animals, your toddler grandchild and you at a child-sized table and chairs make a tea party. Or lay out a towel on the floor and arrange the cups and animals around it for a tea time picnic.

By two years of age your toddler can help you cook.

Establish the ritual of washing hands before handling food. Here are some suggestions for the beginning chef:

• **WASH PRODUCE** Use sturdy ones: apples, oranges, carrots, radishes. You may have a small vegetable brush that is just the right size for him to use.

• **"SHAKE 'EM UP" APPLE SLICES** Slice apples and put them in a resealable plastic bag. Sprinkle in a generous amount of a cinnamon-and-sugar mixture and seal the bag. Chant with your toddler while he shakes:

> *Shake, shake, shake,*
>
> *Shake, shake, shake,*
>
> *Shake your apples,*
>
> *Shake your apples.*

• **SPRINKLE ANYTHING** Try sprinkling a cinnamon-and-sugar mixture on toast, powdered sugar on strawberries, raisins on cereal, or granola on yogurt.

• **GET OUT YOUR COOKIE CUTTERS** Cut your toddler's sandwich, cheese slice, or piece of watermelon into a shape he can recognize.

• **DIP AND TASTE** It is amazing how children will eat what they have dipped. Let them try dipping fruit in yogurt or vegetables in salad dressing.

• MAKE INSTANT OATMEAL He can add the milk or water and stir. After you cook it in the microwave (one minute should do the trick), test to be sure it is not too hot for the toddler.

• PREPARE PANCAKES A toddler can pour in the milk that you have measured and stir the batter. He can drop in raisins, blueberries or cranberries for a tasty addition.

• CLEAN UP TOGETHER For a toddler, this final cooking step just might be the most fun and sets a good example of sharing chores. Sing a clean-up song while you work.

> *Clean up, clean up, clean up, everyone.*
>
> *Clean up, clean up, clean up's lots of fun.*

• HAVE YOUR YOUNG TODDLER HELP put trash into a wastebasket. Give him a damp sponge and show him how to wipe his high chair, the cabinets, or the table. Your older toddler can help to clean the floor. He can put away crayons, paints, or any utensils he has been using. Be sure to thank and compliment him as he works. Within your grandchild's earshot, brag to Grandpa about your helper.

Laurie: I found a small dustpan and brush in my local hardware store—the perfect size for my two-year-old helper. Check out www.forsmallhands.com for other child-sized tools.

In the family room

• PLAY WITH CARS OR TRUCKS and watch your toddler push them around the room. If the truck is large, he may put his teddy bear or a favorite blankie inside for a ride. Sit on the floor with him several feet apart and push the truck back and forth.

• BUILD WITH BLOCKS One of the most versatile toys for young children, blocks "fit" infants, toddlers and preschoolers, too. Toddlers love both soft and hard blocks. Soft blocks can be used to build tall towers to knock down. Wooden blocks can be lined up, stacked or put into containers to dump and refill again and again.

• PULL TOYS ARE FAVORITES If you do not have any pull toys, make your own. Poke a hole in a shoebox and attach a ribbon to it. Can a little stuffed animal or his blankie take a ride? Punch holes in some milk cartons and tie them together to make a train. Tie a scarf around a stuffed kitty to make a leash and go for a walk. An older toddler can even pull a small roller bag…a traveler in training!

• TODDLERS LOVE TO PUSH With a mini-shopping cart, a sofa bolster or a rolled up sleeping bag a toddler can say, "See how strong I am!"

• "LOOK WHAT I CAN CARRY" Toddlers want to prove they can carry large items, sometimes as big as they are. The key to success is to provide lightweight objects, such as:

- a cloth bag stuffed with scarves or crumpled newspaper

- a beach ball

- a large stuffed animal or doll

- an old briefcase or small, empty suitcase

- a large purse in which you tuck a few treasures like a brush or some old keys

• A TODDLER'S URGE TO CLIMB IS HARD TO SATISFY With your careful supervision, he will enjoy:

- scrambling up onto the couch and figuring out how to get off again and again. "Up you go, down you go."

- standing on a footstool. Can he see out the window?

- scrambling onto a pile of couch pillows or large bean bag chairs for a soft rumble tumble.

• FOR A ROLY-POLY TIME Pull your couch pillows and even seat cushions down onto the floor. Have fun playing Peek-A-Boo and gently bouncing on the pillows. It is up to you how far this one will go. How about making a game of putting the couch back together when you are done?

• MAKE A COLORFUL ZIGZAG PATH across the carpet with napkins or felt squares and follow it with a jump, hop or crawl.

- **POST-IT NOTES WILL KEEP YOUR TODDLER BUSY** He may want to stick them on the walls to decorate a room. You can make a game of finding them all and sticking them back into a pile when it is time to clean up.

- **FOR OLDER TODDLERS, RAMP UP THE CHALLENGE** Ask him if he can put a Post-It note *under* the table, *behind* the chair, *on* the doorknob, *next to* the piano? He will be proud to show he knows what those words mean.

- **INTRODUCE FINGER FRIENDS** Using washable markers, draw a tiny face on the index finger of your grandchild and one on your own. Now your friends are ready to talk with each other. Try it with toes for guaranteed giggles.

- **BUILD AN INDY 500 RACEWAY** Uncarpeted floors are the perfect surface for zooming toddlers' cars or for chugging a toy train on an imaginary track.

- **SET UP A BOWLING ALLEY** How many empty plastic bottles can your grandchild knock down by rolling a soft rubber ball?

- **CREATE A PRETEND BEACH DAY** Spread a blue beach towel or tablecloth on the floor. Take turns wading into the "water" and eventually even jumping into it. You might fish from the edge with a drinking straw fishing pole that has a string tied to it, or teach a teddy bear or doll how to swim or float in the water. Could snack time be a beach picnic today? Talk about who lives in the water…a fish, a turtle, a horse? If you have a collection of little plastic animals, have them join you at the beach.

- **DROP CLOTHESPINS** Plunk clothespins into the opening of a plastic jug or bottle. Give it a shake for noisy fun, then dump them out and start again. The larger the size of the opening, the easier it will be for young toddlers. Small openings require more dexterity.

- **PLAY A TODDLER VERSION OF HIDE-AND-SEEK** Ask him if he would like to hide somewhere in this room and you will try to find him. Of course you know exactly where he is hiding, but first check a few wrong places loudly. "Are you in the closet? Behind this big chair? Under the desk?" He will likely burst with anticipation before you find him.

- **TODDLERS ARE GOOD "CLEANER UPPERS"** Let your toddler use your feather duster to help you clean the coffee table, the bookcase or the baseboards. If you need to polish furniture or floors, enlist his help. Slip an old sport sock over his hand and show him how to rub the legs of the table and chairs for a shine. The completion of a job like this is a perfect high-five moment.

In the bedroom, hall or bath

• TOSSING GAME Make a game of tossing inflatable balls (or sandwich-sized plastic bags stuffed with tissue or crumpled newspaper) into a laundry basket. Can he score a three-pointer?

 *Laurie:* The day suddenly turned dark and stormy but I had promised my two-year-old grandson that we would play ball. The solution? I closed all of the bedroom doors along the hall and took the pictures off the walls. Almost instantly, we had an area where nothing could be broken. An added benefit was that the ball was contained and easy to retrieve when it fell through his hands or skidded by as he tried to kick it.

• LAUNDRY BASKET TRAVEL Help your toddler get settled inside the basket, taking along a doll or stuffed animal to pretend that he is going on a trip. With you pulling, the basket slides along on the pretend road or train track.

• CARRYING OBJECTS Toddlers love to move anything they can from one place to another. Make it a game. "How many things can we put in this basket? Now can you put them all on the bed? Do they fit on Grandpa's cozy chair?"

• INDOOR WATER PLAY The bathtub is not just for getting clean. It can also be a soothing, entertaining place to play with water. With cups for pouring, a few rubber duckies, soap bubbles, bath crayons or other water toys, a toddler will be happily occupied until the water gets cold.

⚠ **Safety reminder:** Never leave a child unattended in the bathtub.

• **A BEDTIME SAFARI** Hide a few favorite animals in the child's bedroom. If it is dark, let your grandchild use a flashlight to find the hiding bunny and teddy bear.

• **HAPPY THOUGHTS** As your grandchild is going to sleep, talk about his favorite memory of the day or something funny that happened. As he gets older you might even talk about things that have gone awry.

OUTDOOR PLAY

Open the door for a toddler and she will experience the same excitement an adult might feel at the prospect of going on an African safari. But for her, no need to travel to another continent…no passport required. You can be her guide to the natural wonders in your own back yard or to what is going on in the neighborhood.

Any toddler would relish the life of Dora the Explorer who wanders where she wants, when she wants and without regard to schedules or time. Many of today's harried parents cannot afford the luxury of stopping the clock for their child's moments of discovery. However, grammies know the importance of doing just that and can offer a reassuring antidote to the rushed lifestyle many children experience.

A grammie can follow her own little explorer grandchild on leisurely hunts outside to see what is there—under rocks, around corners, behind trees. This active, unstructured exploring builds a toddler's knowledge bank and stimulates her curiosity as she watches and discusses with you how an ant scurries across the sidewalk or a hummingbird hovers above a blossom. Moreover, outdoor time spent investigating and moving around encourages physical activity, a positive factor in preventing childhood obesity.

You will recall that toddlers do not care about schedules. They move at their own pace and go only as fast as their curiosity and short legs allow.

Cindy: Trips down the driveway to the mailbox could take half an hour as my two-year-old grandson stopped to pick up each stick and examine every pebble. He was teaching me the value of enjoying the journey and smelling the roses.

Here are some ideas for your outdoor adventurer:

• TAKE A WALK Bring along a bag to fill with treasures (acorns, leaves, pieces of tan bark) you have collected.

• ROLL THE BALL Sit on the ground and then roll the ball back and forth, first using your hands and then your feet. The younger the child, the bigger and lighter the ball should be.

• PLAY CATCH Beach balls are the easiest to toss and catch as children of this age develop hand-eye coordination.

• KICK THE BALL Set up two goalposts a few feet apart (lawn chairs work fine), stand back and watch her kick the ball. Cheer as she makes a goal. When she is older, add some obstacles to make it more challenging.

Lynne: The challenge at our house with four little soccer players was maintaining our supply of kickballs. To be sure we had them all, I learned to buy brightly colored ones and had my grandsons count them with me before and after playing outside.

• SAND PLAY AT GRAMMIE'S With a bag of sand from your local hardware store and a large plastic bin, you can create an instant sandbox. Use scoops from detergent boxes, or use plastic bottles, tennis ball containers, funnels, and strainers as tools to dig a hole, mix up a bucket of sand cakes or build a castle.

OOPS! If you store your sandbox outside, it is wise to cover it with a sturdy lid to keep out unwanted critters.

• **BUBBLES MAKE ANY DAY A CELEBRATION**   Use a plastic strawberry basket as a bubble blower. Dip it into a shallow pan of soapy solution and wave it in the air as you try to catch or count the oodles of bubbles. Your grandchild will love watching, chasing and eventually bursting them.

 TIP: Make a quick bubble solution by adding eight tablespoons of liquid dish detergent to one quart of water. Keep a towel handy for a soap-in-the-eye emergency or quick mop-up.

• **PILE UP AUTUMN LEAVES** Crunchy leaves are fun to walk through and jump into. If your grandchild will be visiting soon, save a pile for her to play in.

• **IS IT TRASH DAY IN YOUR NEIGHBORHOOD?** Children love sorting and can help you toss items into the appropriate recycling container. Listen and watch together as the garbage trucks come closer working their way up the street.

• **WELCOME RAINY DAYS** With umbrellas, raincoats, Froggie boots or Crocs, toddlers are all set for puddle walks. Who else is out in the rain—worms, snails, birds and maybe even the mailman? It is also fun to plop pebbles, leaves and sticks into puddles.

OOPS! If you want to join your toddler in the splashing, dig out your own rubber shoes or prepare to get your feet wet!

• SING THOSE CLASSIC RAIN SONGS As the drops keep falling, sing:

Rain, rain, go away.

Come again another day.

Little Johnny wants to play.

It's raining, it's pouring, the old man is snoring.

He jumped in bed and bumped his head,

And couldn't get up in the morning.

Laurie: While traveling with my toddler grandson I tucked in an inflatable beach ball, to use rain or shine, indoors or out. I let him help me blow it up and we were able to play ball without breaking a thing—even in a hotel room.

• PLAY SUNNY DAY SHADOW TAG Try to "catch" your grandchild's shadow and then it is her turn to chase yours. Just being aware of her own shadow "following" her can be a momentous discovery. Can she run and see if her own shadow can keep up? Where does that shadow go when she hides behind the tree? Does the tree have a shadow? What else has a shadow?

• TRY CHASE GAMES Remember your children's delight when you played chase games? "I'm gonna get you...I'm gonna get you," concluding with a hug and kiss. Now, "Can you catch Grammie? Oh no, you caught me." All this running around is best outdoors but can work inside, too, if there is enough room.

 • MAKE A TRAIN Line up a few cardboard boxes big enough for your grandchild to sit in. Paint or decorate them with your young artist. Connect them with clothesline rope or twine and your backyard choo-choo is ready to be pulled.

• DRAW WITH SIDEWALK CHALK This is an easy and colorful way to create art on your driveway or sidewalk. A rain shower or a quick squirt with the hose will wash it away.

- **PICK A BOUQUET** Toddlers don't need elegant roses; dandelions and other flowering weeds work just fine. The greater the variety of blooms, the more chances your toddler will have to discover different smells, colors and textures. Can she blow dandelion puffs? As they float away, make a wish.

- **TODDLERS LOVE TO WATER PLANTS** A small watering can or plastic measuring cup may be just the right size for young gardeners. Set your plants where a few spills would not matter.

- **PRACTICE THOSE NEW WALKING SKILLS** Toddlers will repeatedly trudge up and then run down a grassy slope. Join in…great exercise for you both.

> *Cindy:* While spending the day at a park with my grandsons and their mom, I showed the boys how to roll down a gentle hill. I could hear my daughter laughing as she took more pictures of me than she took of them. I guess she didn't know I still had it in me.

- **FILL THE BIRD FEEDER** Who do you think will come for dinner? Will they come if you are standing too close?

- **OLDER TODDLERS CAN BALANCE** Stand by as they get more daring in finding their balance on a curb or low wall. Some will try a two-footed jump from a step or curb over and over again. Unlike busy moms, grammies are in no hurry to move on. They can take the time to appreciate the show.

- **PAINT WITH WATER** Grab a two- or three-inch wide paintbrush, set out a shallow container of water and invite your grandchild to "paint" your porch railing, sidewalk or patio furniture. Finished painting? Try following the trail of wet footprints along the sidewalk before they magically disappear in the sun.

- **SIT OUTSIDE TOGETHER** On a warm evening listen to the symphony of sounds, such as crickets, frogs and barking dogs. Show your grandchild how to make "deer ears" by cupping her hands behind her ears to focus the sound. Can she make the sound too? See if you can guess which insect or animal she is imitating.

• **LEARN THE LANGUAGE OF ASTRONOMY** What shape is the moon tonight? How many stars are there? Can we see the Milky Way?

Jan: As a child, I loved gazing at the night sky and imagining star pictures. So starting when my grandchildren were toddlers, I enjoyed taking them on night walks. We sang "Twinkle, Twinkle" and chanted "Star light, star bright." They were astronomers in the making.

• **PRETEND YOUR BACK YARD IS A FARM** Which corner is the horse corral? Set out a pail of water for an animal your grandchild can imagine is thirsty. Can she make a pig sound? Did we hear a cow over there? Where should we keep the chickens?

• **GO ON A CIRCLE SEARCH** Can your grandchild spot circles outside, such as a wreath, a door knob, a car tire or flower blossom? Carry on this game inside the house, too, or when traveling in the car. Try looking for other familiar shapes—triangles and squares.

• **MAKE A NATURE WINDOW** Gather flat natural items: flower petals, fall leaves, blades of grass. Ask your grandchild to place them on a sheet of wax paper. Then she can add a few scraps of ribbon, tissue paper or some glitter. When they are arranged, put a second sheet of wax paper on top. Get out your iron—an unknown appliance and wonder to most children these days—and set it on Low. Protect the iron by putting a paper towel between it and the wax paper. Slowly iron over the layers, pressing, to melt the wax papers together for a beautiful picture.

• **ENJOY A SNOWY DAY** Dress warmly and turn a snowy day into a play day. Do you remember lying in the soft snow, moving your arms and legs like windshield wipers to make snow angels? Tromp around and play Follow My Footsteps or share the fun of building a snowman.

• **TAKE A SLED RIDE** Pulling your bundled-up toddler will give you a workout, and she will have a view of the winter wonderland. Stop now and then to look around and listen. What does she hear?

- **CLEAR A PATH IN THE SNOW** With a child-sized broom or shovel, your grandchild can help you with your chores. For extra fun, can she make a pile of snow to jump in?

- **BRING THE OUTDOORS IN** On bitter cold days in snow country, fill up your kitchen sink with snow. Forget the snowsuit...your toddler will only need a pair of mittens to pat or make a snowball.

Lynne: Some of my grandchildren live where it doesn't snow, so imagine their excitement when we brought them a cooler full of snow from our trip to the ski slopes. We dumped the cooler in their yard and they giggled as they made snow-balls and a mini-snowman.

THE NEIGHBORHOOD AND BEYOND

There are many places you can take your toddler near your home that re-quire no special planning or arrangements. The destination does not have to be extraordinary like an amusement park; for this age, simple is better. A toddler wants instant gratification with no long drives. A short visit or experience and home again is what he is after. On your regular round of errands, you can add one of these field trips:

Easy outings

- **VISIT THE GROCERY STORE** This is not a fill-your-pantry trip but an exploration of all the different foods people eat. From the colors and shapes on display, he can choose an apple, count the bananas or select the vegetables for dinner. Enticing aromas may lure you to the bakery department. Maybe you will be offered a cookie...hopefully you have had lunch first.

- **MAIL A LETTER** Write a letter or draw a picture to send to a relative or friend. Address and close the envelope, put on the stamp, find the neighbor-hood mailbox, pull the handle, drop the envelope in and watch it disappear. Talk about where that letter goes next and what fun it is to give someone a special surprise.

• GO TO A PET SHOP See the different animals and their babies and talk about the difference between a kitten and a cat, a puppy and a dog.

• REMEMBER THE PARK If it has been a while since you spent time in your local park, you will be amazed by the new design of playground equipment and the safer play surfaces. Even if it is a park with no play structures, your grandchild can enjoy the open area for running around.

 TIP: Getting a toddler to leave a park can be challenging. "Five more minutes" can go on and on. When you really must head home, letting him push his own stroller along the sidewalk may be a great way to get him moving.

• SHOP AT THE FARMERS' MARKET If your town has one, it is a good place to see foods close to their natural state. Children, these days, think all carrots are "mini" and come in plastic bags. Can you find carrots or beets with tops attached or potatoes of different colors? Your toddler can help you select some fruits or vegetables. Often vendors give out samples. You may find your toddler is willing to taste something new…and like it!

• VISIT A CONSTRUCTION SITE Stop to watch the many workers maneuver big trucks and cement mixers.

• VIEW PLANES TAKING OFF AND LANDING An airport cell phone waiting area makes a perfect parking spot.

• STOP AT YOUR NEIGHBORHOOD FIRE STATION See the trucks and a firefighter or two. It is best to call ahead on their non-emergency number to schedule a visit.

• RIDE A LOCAL BUS Let your toddler give the driver the money, choose the seat and together you can look out the window for landmarks along the way.

• GO TO A COMMUNITY LIBRARY OR BOOKSTORE These are terrific places to spend an hour or so. Check your library website or call local bookstores for hours and special events for children. Sit and read together or plan to attend a scheduled story time.

With a bit more time or planning

 TIP: See page 32 for advice about a Go Bag for outings with grandchildren. What do you need today—diapers and wipes, drinks and snacks, change of clothes, hats and sunscreen, extra jacket, first aid basics?

• TAKE A COUNTRY DRIVE Be on the lookout for horses, cows, sheep or goats in the field.

• VISIT A STABLE Have fun watching the riders in the ring. If your grandchild seems interested, ask if you can step inside the stable, pet the horse's nose or feed Seabiscuit a carrot.

• DO YOU LIVE NEAR A POND, LAKE OR STREAM? Watching for minnows, turtles or salamanders can be a wonderful way to spend an unstructured afternoon. Some parks allow feeding the ducks and geese. No wildlife here today? Not to worry...children of all ages have an insatiable desire to throw pebbles, leaves and twigs into any body of water.

Safety Reminder: Any activity near water requires constant supervision especially deep water where a child could slip and fall in or venture out too far. This is a good time to reinforce the AAP's Touch Rule: Near or in water, keep your child close enough to touch. If you live close to a pool, the ocean, a lake or a swiftly flowing stream, you will need to make the safety guidelines very clear. There is danger here!

• WANT A DAY AT THE BEACH? Pack up sunhat, sunscreen, a change of clothes, diapers, beach blanket, towel, sand toys, bathing suit, a snack and lots of drinking water. With your more flexible grammie schedule, you and your toddler can enjoy a leisurely day collecting seashells, digging in the sand, picnicking or playing along the shore.

Cindy: Did you know that if you sprinkle baby powder on a child after you have toweled him dry, the sand brushes off like magic? It worked on my grandson even though he was covered in sand from head to toe.

• LOOK FOR UPCOMING CHILDREN'S EVENTS Consult your local newspaper or the internet for events such as fairs or puppet shows. Many offerings sound tempting, but are they appropriate for your toddler? Check the details.

• TAKE HIM TO A MUSIC OR MOVEMENT CLASS Some classes especially for toddlers are offered by town recreation departments.

• VISIT THE WEBSITES OF MUSEUMS AND SCIENCE CENTERS Visit or call them for current exhibits and ask if they are appropriate for toddlers of your grandchild's age.

What's next?

Ready or not, toddlers move on. They are treasures that sparkle with the enthusiasm of discovery and we want to show them off to our friends like fine jewelry. They are so cute, so increasingly confident in their new skills and so verbal. Although it requires extra energy to keep up with them, toddlers accessorize our lives with unconditional love and abundant laughter, sloppy kisses and excitement about the otherwise everyday things of life.

TIP: To preserve these memories in a tangible way, collect toddler treasures in an album or a shoebox: a lock of hair, a first drawing, cute things she said and photos of milestones. As your grandchild grows, pull out the album and go through it together to recall times you have shared.

Just when you think you have become an expert at how to play with a toddler, he surprises you by arriving suddenly (or so it seems) at a new stage. He develops new interests and is honing new skills. It is time to gear up and move forward with your grandchild who, at two-and-a-half, is now entering the world of a preschooler.

CHAPTER 4

YOUR PRESCHOOLER GRANDCHILD
(2 1/2-years to 5-years-old)

HOW LUCKY YOU ARE! DIAPERS ARE A THING OF THE PAST (or soon will be), naps are once a day if at all, and you now have many more ways to enjoy time with your preschooler grandchild.

WHAT IS A PRESCHOOLER LIKE?

The preschool period in a child's life, as defined here, covers two-and-a-half years. That is a lot of territory chronologically and developmentally...from the younger preschooler who cannot keep up, to the older one who moves almost as fast as you. One significant difference you will remember between these years and toddlerhood is that a preschooler can amuse himself for longer periods of time. He also requires less help from you than he did previously because he can do more for himself.

Preschoolers' social skills are expanding as they observe and interact with other children and adults in their daily routines. This is the time they typically learn their letters, numbers and colors. Although not growing as fast physically as in their first two years, they are developing emotionally and gaining more self-control. It is at this age children begin to realize that society has certain rules which everyone is expected to follow.

A preschooler can communicate his ideas with greater clarity now and exhibits more of his unique personality and identity as an individual. These are the so-called Magic Years when a child immerses himself in fantasy play and his imagination flourishes. If you have a fairy or a friendly dragon hiding within you, now is the time to let it out to play.

Times have changed

Life is a bit more serious for today's children. At some level even small children sense the generally heightened awareness of the human impact on the earth. They know about recycling, saving water and endangered animals. Many are able to discuss healthy eating habits and, because of the prevalence of food allergies, they respect special diets of others. They know about the effects of overexposure to the sun and are used to being slathered with sunscreen. With dispensers of antibacterial soap everywhere, preschoolers are frequent hand washers and know why it is important.

Children today are supervised more closely by adults than they were decades ago. Their play space is often limited to the yard, they have play dates arranged rather than joining in spontaneous play in the neighborhood and they are delivered by car to most destinations. With Amber Alerts and more sensational publicity given to crimes against children, many of today's parents tend to hover, thus the term "helicopter parenting." It describes the behavior of anxious parents who supervise every aspect of their child's life to an extreme.

A young child's day may be tightly scheduled with preschool, daycare, music lessons, structured sports programs and even academics. This is partly because many families depend on two incomes and need to cover a child's care throughout a full day. It may also be due to parental anxiety that, if children are not enrolled in a myriad of classes, they may not measure up to their peers when it is time for kindergarten. It goes without saying that parents have always wanted their children to do well. Today, however, many parents' ambitions for their children have reached a new level due to the pressures of our overly competitive society.

And finally, this generation of preschoolers is bombarded with television and movie characters every waking hour. They are printed on his pajamas, toothbrush, underwear and backpack. They are relentlessly featured as toys and birthday party themes. From blinking shoes to sequined T-shirts, everything has a logo. Because the media convince preschoolers what they want is what they need, preschoolers are robbed of the freedom to make individual choices. What can a grammie do to solve this troubling problem?

Some things never change

In spite of the differences in the world for young children today, their needs remain the same. Your grandchild needs the same kind of love and attention you gave his parent. He needs free time—time to explore, experiment, make choices and make mistakes. He needs time to play. His play is his work and it is how he learns and makes sense of his world. Young children deserve time to be children.

A GRAMMIE'S ROLE IN HEALTHY DEVELOPMENT

Parents having one-on-one time with children is a limited luxury in many homes today. This is where you come in, Grammie, by simply making yourself available. Bring out the crayons, blocks and other open-ended toys. Be attentive and patient answering her endless "Why?" questions. Feeling energetic? Play tag, throw a ball or take her for a walk. Most of all, be there for her…someone she can talk to and laugh with. Your time, attention and unconditional affection are the most important gifts you can give her.

A word about pacing

Though your grandchild may no longer take naps, she still needs some down time. As you remember with your own children, things go better with a balance of both quiet and lively activities during the day. If she has been corralled in a classroom or held captive in her car seat for a long time, she may need space to run off some of that excess energy. Conversely, if she has just finished an active morning at the park, suggest she choose a puzzle to work on or a book for the two of you to read together.

Of course, you will want to maintain her regular rhythm of meals and possibly naps, when she is with you. But you can offer her a less structured day with lots of choices—something her at-home routine may not allow. When possible, let her choose not only what to do, but in what order she would like to do it. This shows her that you value her opinion and builds her sense of importance. Does she want to go to the park in the morning or in the afternoon? Does she want to ride her Big Wheel to the mailbox before or after her lunch? Shall we read the book on the floor or on the couch?

WHAT THE EXPERTS SAY ABOUT SCREEN TIME

The AAP consistently recommends limiting media use of all types to a total of no more than two hours a day for preschoolers. It is not just television. Screens of all sizes—computers, handheld games and smart phones—count in the screen time limit. Keep your eye on the clock even with television games like bowling and baseball which are more interactive and physical.

What about "educational" television shows designed for children? It is true that short doses of these programs may result in some superficial rote learning which preschoolers can then parrot back. However, this type of "learning" lacks depth of understanding and integration of concepts.

We continue to discover more about how children learn. Anthropologist Melvin Konner in *The Evolution of Childhood* concludes that play is nature's primary means for developing the brain. Now more than ever, in this high tech society, children who sit passively in front of television are robbed of valuable playtime. Furthermore, excessive time in front of a screen can impair a child's learning potential, lead to dependency on passive entertainment and promote an addiction to fast-paced, constantly changing visual stimulation. Attention spans should lengthen as children age but if youngsters become overly accustomed to short action/short response scenarios, they may be unable to hold a thought or concentrate for very long.

Face-to-face interaction with an adult is critical. You cannot fight the influence of screens completely, but you can offer your grandchild a healthy, fun alternative for both his mind and body and a haven from the onslaught of commercialism when he is with you. Turn off any and all screens and be fully present to play with your grandchild…you will both reap the benefits.

EQUIPMENT

Just the basics

If you stock your home with the items below, you can reduce what a child's parents need to pack when he comes to visit. Remind them he will need extra clothing, special blanket, toothbrush and medications, if needed.

For sleeping:

• BED Younger preschoolers may still need a guard rail. Older ones are likely to prefer using a sleeping bag or bedding on the floor.

• SHEETS, WATERPROOF MATTRESS COVER, BLANKETS AND A PILLOW A backup set of sheets and a waterproof mattress cover are good "just in case." Preschoolers like pillows to cuddle along with their favorite stuffed animals.

• NIGHTLIGHT Your grandchild may feel more secure at your house overnight using a nightlight even if he does not need one at home.

For toileting:

• POTTY CHAIR OR POTTY SEAT Either item makes toileting easier for a preschooler.

• DIAPERS AND WIPES, IF NEEDED Young preschoolers may still use regular diapers, especially overnight. Some may have graduated to today's pull-up diapers which are like padded disposable underpants. Ask parents for their advice on what to buy.

Cindy: When my grandson was newly potty trained, we were on an outing and he needed to make a "pit stop." He was too short to stand and reach above the toilet edge so, rather than awkwardly hold him, I had him stand on MY feet for a little extra height...this tip has saved the day with all of my grandsons.

For bathing:

- NON-TEAR SOAP AND SHAMPOO
- BATH TOYS
- NON-SLIP MAT
- STEPSTOOL

For feeding:

- BOOSTER OR YOUTH CHAIR
- SMALL-SIZED PLASTIC PLATES,

CUPS AND UTENSILS

- SIPPY CUPS
- BIBS

For traveling:

• CAR SEAT It must meet legal requirements and fit correctly in your car. Ask parents or your local police station for help with installation. Car seats must face backward until children reach two years or the maximum height and weight limits for the seat. See www.aaa.com for the latest regulations.

• STROLLER For those times when he is just too tired to walk further, today's so-called umbrella strollers work well. They are also easy to use and store.

• BACKPACK OR TOTE BAG This is recommended for all the miscellaneous items needed on outings, including diapers, extra clothing, snacks and a few books for the road.

For playing:

• TOYS Good choices are blocks, books, puzzles, balls, dolls and/or small figures, small vehicles and simple sock puppets.

• ART SUPPLIES Have the basics on hand: crayons, markers and paper of all kinds.

Nice-to-haves

These are the extras that make child-tending easier, especially for grandchildren who visit regularly.

• RIDING TOYS

• BOARD GAMES, PLAYING CARDS, DOMINOES

• ADDITIONAL ART SUPPLIES

• CDS OF CHILDREN'S MUSIC

• STUFFED ANIMALS

• MAGNIFYING GLASS

• FLASHLIGHT

• OUTDOOR EQUIPMENT Sand toys, kite, bat and ball, child-sized broom, rake and snow shovel

HOW A PRESCHOOLER GROWS:

A Refresher Course

A preschooler today follows the same development milestones your children did thirty years ago, in spite of the current rush toward early academic achievement. She may have two years under her belt at "KinderCollege" and be able to get to apps on your smart phone faster than you but, nevertheless, she is still a preschooler and the following chart will help you remember what to expect.

Lynne: Preschoolers are just like snowflakes: each one is unique. As a teacher of three-year-olds, I saw a wide range of abilities and behaviors displayed by normal, healthy children of the same chronological age. Who is a "Three?" He or she may be as verbal as a four-year-old, as co-operative and conforming as a typical three-year-old, and yet be struggling with the lack of physical coordination of a much younger child!

YOUR 2 1/2-YEAR-OLD PRESCHOOLER MAY...	REMINDERS AND TIPS
Be inflexible. This is the peak age of negativism.	Distract and redirect.
Rarely sit still.	Give her space and time to run, jump, climb and throw or kick a rubber ball.
Like to play Hide-and-Seek.	Define the play space and count loudly to ten.
Understand simple time concepts such as *after* and *before*.	Use these words often. Now she will get it when you say, "We will go for yogurt *after* your nap."
Grasp physical relationships of *in, on, under* and *beside*.	Play a game: can she climb *in* the box, *on* the couch, hide *under* the table, and sit *beside* Grandpa?
Have difficulty making decisions.	Limit choices. "Do you want to wear your fuzzy jacket or your hoody today?"
Scribble with circular motion.	Give her large sheets of paper and fat crayons.
Express affection openly.	Enjoy those special kisses and leg hugs.
Be less egocentric as she approaches age three.	Praise her when she shares her crackers with a friend.

YOUR 3-YEAR-OLD PRESCHOOLER MAY...	REMINDERS AND TIPS
Recognize and name colors.	Remember guessing games like "I spy with my little eye something green?" Can he find it?
Want to do things for himself.	Allow extra time to let him try. Support his efforts and use encouraging words.
Be able to take his clothes off, but needs help putting them on.	Let him do as much as he can but step in to assist if he gets frustrated.
Show dramatic increase in coordination.	Get on your running shoes and try to keep pace with him.
Use "we" instead of "me" and be more friendly and positive now.	Include him in social gatherings. Let others enjoy him, too.
Be more willing to try something new.	Build on his growing curiosity and openness. Introduce new people, places and things.
Have a vocabulary of about 500 words.	Read to him; act out stories and talk, talk, talk.
Wake during the night with bad dreams.	Hold and calm him, talk briefly about the dream and stay with him while he settles back down to sleep.
Want to copy what he sees others doing.	If it is safe, let him give it a try. If you are washing the dishes, can he give you a hand?
Take everything literally.	When you talk about "putting a bug in Grandpa's ear," he will want to take a peek. Explain that it is just an expression.

YOUR 3 1/2-YEAR-OLD PRESCHOOLER MAY...	REMINDERS AND TIPS
Be shy at one moment and over-bold the next.	Respect these inconsistencies. It is part of being three-and-a-half years old.
May bite her nails, stutter, frequently blink, tremble or stumble.	Be patient, supportive and do not worry. Soon she will feel more in control and under control.
Be able to cut across a sheet of paper with scissors.	Give her an old catalog and sit with her while she practices cutting.
Fall apart emotionally.	Take a deep breath and stay calm. Suggest another activity to distract her.
Enjoy games like Tag and understand the rules.	Set up the rules together and play. Take turns being "it."
Enjoy more complicated art projects that involve multiple steps.	Set out a variety of art materials and see what she creates.
Be able to do two things at once (sing while drawing, rhyme words while dressing).	Play rhyming games as you hike together or sing while picking up toys.
Live at times in a fantasy world. If she says she is a dog, she believes she really IS a dog.	Encourage her imaginative play. Are you keeping a journal of her imaginary friends?
As she approaches age four, display more coordination with new skills like skipping, ice skating or pumping the swing.	Give her plenty of opportunities to practice and show off. Stand by in case she needs help.

YOUR 4-YEAR-OLD PRESCHOOLER MAY...	REMINDERS AND TIPS
Be loud, daring, egocentric, boastful, tough or defiant.	Establish safe and firm boundaries, knowing he may push them. Remember that four-year-olds like to talk big.
Have a vocabulary of about 1,000 words.	He may deliberately use words that are rude or shocking. Minimize the power of negative words by correcting him but not overreacting.
Experiment with "bathroom" talk.	Ignore the talk. It is normal for the age. If you do not react or if you confine this talk to the bathroom, it is less fun for him.
Clown around and be silly.	Be silly too. Can you make a funny face, recite a goofy poem or walk like a duck?
Be too chatty during meals.	Tell him "When you have eaten five bites, you can tell me the rest of the story."
Constantly ask, "Why?"	Respond but encourage him to think of answers, too.
Be demanding and sassy.	Acknowledge his feelings and suggest a better way.
Tell preposterous tales which he believes.	Respond with "hmmm" or "really" to let him know you are listening and thinking it over.

YOUR 4 1/2-YEAR-OLD PRESCHOOLER MAY...	REMINDERS AND TIPS
Have better control of his emotions.	Keep routines predictable and let him know what is planned.
Be curious about how his body works. "What happens to the food I eat?" "What do my bones look like?"	Answer questions simply. There are some great books on these topics for preschoolers.
Be very active and play hard—may gallop, hop on one foot, climb high on play equipment, and pump on swings.	Take him outside where he has room to really run and play. If you join in, you will get a good workout, too.
Be proud of his accomplishments and look for approval.	Notice what he has done. "Wow! You picked up all your toys without a reminder. Your room is so orderly now."
Have better small motor coordination, color with a purpose and draw people with a head, body and arms.	Display his artwork in a prominent place or keep a scrapbook of his best drawings. Remember to date them.
Share and take turns more readily.	Simple card and board games are a helpful way to practice and reinforce taking turns.
Want to help with real chores.	Could he help set the table, fold the laundry or feed the cat?
Want to discuss favorite subjects ad infinitum.	If you do not know much about outer space or dinosaurs, Google it before he comes next time.
Be wrestling with some big questions like birth and death.	Be sensitive to what he is really asking. Keep your answers brief.

What about gender?

The difference in the way boys and girls play becomes more apparent during the preschool years. Although there are exceptions, boys seem drawn to anything with wheels, to building activities and to traditional masculine roles like firemen, sailors and pirates in their fantasy play. They tend to be boisterous and active.

Girls usually show longer attention spans with small motor activities, are more aware of others, enjoy playing house and taking care of stuffed animals and dolls. They are aware of their clothing and how their hair is styled.

This said, however, whether your grandchild is male or female, give them opportunities to explore all aspects of play.

ACTIVITIES PRESCHOOLERS ENJOY, ROOM BY ROOM

Fun in the kitchen

Can children as young as two-and-a-half or three actually help with cooking? Absolutely! They want to participate in kitchen tasks. With your guidance and patience, preschoolers gain confidence as cooks.

These days with so many two-career families, there may be little time available for meal preparation. Parents on tight schedules may have to resort to takeout, microwave entrees and fast food. At your house, however, cooking can be an opportunity for relaxed fun with your grandchild. Some excellent cookbooks like *Pretend Soup and Other Real Recipes* by Mollie Katzen and Ann L. Henderson are available for use with preschoolers but your own simple recipes can work well, too.

....

OOPS! Any cooking or kitchen play activity with water or food has the potential to be messy. It is hard to believe how much flour there is in only one cup until it lands on your floor during enthusiastic stirring. If you worry about spills, put a plastic cloth under your work space.

....

Before you begin

Now is a good time to reinforce hand washing not only before handling food but also to prevent the spread of colds and flu. Playfully singing about this healthy routine works well. Experts say that to clean those little hands thoroughly you need to scrub during the entire time it takes to sing Happy Birthday or one of the following songs.

Remember **Popeye, the Sailor Man?** Sing it with these words:

I am a bubble machine.

I scrubble and bubble them clean.

I scrubble and bubble and scrubble and bubble,

I am a bubble machine.

Or sing to the tune of **Here We Go 'Round the Mulberry Bush:**

Over the top, between the fingers,

Over the top, between the fingers,

Over the top, between the fingers,

That's how we wash our hands.

At the sink

Place a sturdy chair with its back toward the sink so your grandchild can stand safely by your side as you work.

Children can help you:

- Scrub vegetables, such as turnips, parsnips and carrots.

- Wash durable fruit like apples, oranges and grapes.

- Snap green beans.

- Break apart cauliflower and broccoli.

- Rinse lettuce, dry it in the spinner and tear into pieces for salad.

- Crack eggs.

Jan: My four-year-old granddaughter loved cracking the eggs for the cake we were making. Uh-oh...more shell than eggs went in! I soon learned to have her crack one at a time into a small bowl so we had a chance to rescue any stray shells before adding eggs to the batter.

Skill Building for the Sous-Chef

Preschoolers can:

• MEASURE INGREDIENTS Does the recipe call for a pinch of salt, a quarter teaspoon of baking soda or a cup of milk?

• POUR INGREDIENTS such as flour, sugar, and liquids from cup to bowl.

 Jan: My twin grandchildren learned a lot about measuring and pouring when we practiced with uncooked beans. You can use lentils or rice, too. I put out a large plastic container, measuring spoons, small cups, a funnel and scoopers. With a cloth underneath the container, clean-up was easy. When the beans served their usefulness as "toys," I simply rinsed them and made bean soup.

• PRACTICE MIXING, STIRRING AND WHISKING

• GREASE BAKING PANS OR COOKIE SHEETS Try painting on the oil or melted butter with a pastry brush.

• SPREAD WITH A BUTTER KNIFE

• CUT SOFT FRUITS AND COOKED VEGETABLES with a plastic or table knife.

• PEEL TANGERINES AND HARD-BOILED EGGS WITH THEIR FINGERS or use a peeler for vegetables.

TIP: Preschoolers can be picky eaters. When they have prepared food themselves, they are more likely to give it a try.

Cooking projects for preschoolers

• STIRRING DRY INGREDIENTS FOR GRANOLA

• MAKING CINNAMON TOAST STEP-BY-STEP Your grandchild can push down the toaster button, spread the butter, make a cinnamon-and-sugar mixture, and sprinkle it on the toast.

• DIPPING SLICED APPLES in a cinnamon-and-sugar mixture for a special snack.

• SLICING HARD-BOILED EGGS with an egg slicer.

• MAKING DESSERTS FROM A MIX: instant pudding, cakes, or muffins.

Laurie: My two-and-a-half year old grandson and I were so busy playing in our hideaway under the kitchen table that we forgot the pizzas until they were burned to a crisp. He was ready to cry until we began to laugh at all the hullabaloo: we set off the smoke alarm, Grandpa came running, the dog was barking. My grandson recalls this big flop much more often than he mentions our cooking successes.

• FROSTING YOUR HOMEMADE SUGAR COOKIES (slice-and-bake are great when time is short) and decorating them with sugar sprinkles, raisins or chopped nuts.

• SPREADING CREAM CHEESE, PEANUT BUTTER, HONEY OR JAM on bread or bagels.

• USING COOKIE CUTTERS to make seasonal shapes or alphabet letters out of cheese slices or soft bread.

Retro but fun

Introduce the old fashioned kitchen gadgets that required muscles not motors. Talk about the times when not everything was mixed up in a food processor or popped into the microwave. With your supervision, your grandchild can:

• SQUEEZE LEMONS OR ORANGES to make lemonade or orange juice the old-fashioned way.

• PEEL POTATOES and after cooking, mash them by hand. Let him add butter and a little milk.

Cindy: For a surprise lunch, I served "Sandwich Puzzles." I made the pieces by using a cookie cutter to cut a simple shape out of the middle of a sandwich. Then I cut the outer section of the bread into a few pieces and separated them on the plate. The kids loved trying to put the pieces back together before gobbling them up.

• GRIND CRANBERRIES WITH A HAND GRINDER, attached to a table edge. Your grandchild can wash the cranberries, drain them in a colander and pour them into the grinder. Turn the handle and listen for the pop-pop-popping sound. Grind unpeeled quartered oranges and add them along with some sugar for a tasty, fresh cranberry relish.

OOPS! Hand grinders may leak, and cranberry juice will stain. Wipe up spills immediately. Use club soda to remove stains on clothes and towels.

• SIFT FLOUR WITH A HAND SIFTER

• USE AN OLD-STYLE EGG BEATER to mix scrambled eggs.

• HUSK CORN outdoors on a summer day.

• CORE, COOK AND MASH APPLES for yummy apple sauce. Add a little cinnamon for flavor. Eat warm or cold.

Pretend parties with Grammie

The kitchen is also a place for make believe.

• PLAN YOUR OWN TEA PARTY Have your grandchild make finger sandwiches, set out little cookies, or cut pieces of fruit. A miniature tea set allows him to be the perfect host as he pours the "tea" (maybe water or lemonade) and passes the food.

• COOK UP A MAKE-BELIEVE STEW Hand your preschooler a large plastic bowl and spatula to "stir" an imaginary mixture. Dump in a cup of "magic powder," a little "water," and see what else he might like to add. Soon the bowl will be filled with such delicious, far-fetched ingredients as seahorses, rainbows and dinosaur eggs. When it is well mixed, invite a teddy bear to have a "taste."

• PLAY RESTAURANT With you as the guest and your grandchild as the waiter, the imaginary ordering begins. "Do you serve pizza?" you ask. "Of course we do—with lots of ice cream!" He can serve you on paper plates and then bus the table. Ask for the bill and do not forget to tip.

• MAKE A HIDEOUT With a sheet over your kitchen table, your grandchild will have a private retreat for his favorite stuffed animals or a parking garage for his cars and trucks. If you are lucky, maybe you will be invited to join him there for a picnic.

For that special occasion

To prepare for the event, let him help:

• SET THE TABLE BY CHOOSING THE PLACEMATS, folding the napkins and counting the number of spoons or forks.

• MAKE A CENTERPIECE as an art project or with flowers from the yard (dandelions accepted).

• MAKE PLACE CARDS and decide who sits where.

• INVITE DINERS TO THE TABLE with a dinner bell or say "Dinner is served."

• BLOW OUT THE CANDLES at the end of the meal.

Before you leave the kitchen

Include your grandchild in the clean-up process.

• BUS THE PLATES

• SPONGE OFF THE COUNTER

• RINSE UNBREAKABLE DISHES in sudsy water.

• HELP LOAD THE DISHWASHER

• PUT AWAY SILVERWARE INTO THEIR RIGHT COMPARTMENTS

• SWEEP THE FLOOR

• RECYCLE plastics, paper, glass and Styrofoam into the proper collection containers.

Set a timer to see how long it takes to finish the job together and whistle while you work. You will leave behind a tidy room, and your children will bless you for encouraging good habits in their children.

In the family room

Preschoolers thrive on activity. They are ready to do and ready to go. If the weather keeps you indoors or if you and your grandchild just prefer to spend the day inside, there is still lots to do.

• WHERE DO THE ANIMALS LIVE? With a few pieces of fabric, a towel or construction paper, you can create a whole animal habitat. Spread out something green for a grassy base, then bring out those little animals and decide who would live here. Do the same with blue to represent water. Who belongs in the ocean…the cow or the dolphin? Your grandchild may want to take it further and create the African plains or a world for dinosaurs.

• PLAY MAILMAN After closing doors to a few rooms in your house, let your grandchild sort your junk mail, old magazines or envelopes he has addressed to people he pretends live behind those doors. Using a cloth laundry bag or handled shopping bag as his carrier, he can slip his note to Grandpa under your bedroom door or mail for you under the door to the kitchen pantry.

• PLAY HIDE-AND-SEEK Set some boundaries to limit the hiding area. Close your eyes while he hides, count to ten before starting to hunt and then shout, "Ready or not, here I come!" Do not be surprised if he always hides in the same place. Next it is his turn to find you.

• GO ON A HUNT Hide a number of objects like plastic eggs, little cars or blocks inside the family room and then say, "Go!" Give him clues, such as "You are nearer" or "You are warmer," as he closes in on a hidden object. Then it is his turn to hide the objects and give you the clues.

• CARD GAMES A regular deck of cards can be used to identify numbers and suits, play matching games, Crazy Eights or Go Fish. Children's card games such as Old Maid and Animal Rummy can be played with preschoolers and older children together.

....

 TIP: As a cardholder for little hands, set a shoebox inside its own cover and stand the cards up between the lid and the box so he can see them and you cannot.

....

• **BOARD GAMES** As you play simple board games, just the two of you, help him learn the rules. Skills like taking turns, counting, using a spinner, moving from space to space and rolling dice can be practiced together.

• **PLAY SCHOOL** The necessary props are easily gathered: a child-sized table and chairs, books, pencils and paper tablets to do his "homework." Who are the students? Surely there are some dolls and stuffed animals that need a lesson or two—or maybe you do!

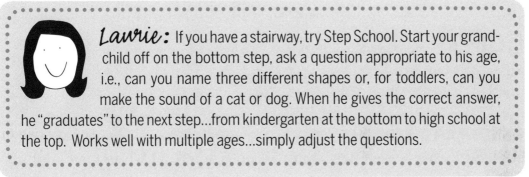

Laurie: If you have a stairway, try Step School. Start your grandchild off on the bottom step, ask a question appropriate to his age, i.e., can you name three different shapes or, for toddlers, can you make the sound of a cat or dog. When he gives the correct answer, he "graduates" to the next step...from kindergarten at the bottom to high school at the top. Works well with multiple ages...simply adjust the questions.

• **GET OUT THE PUPPETS** Puppet play is often a good way for a child to express his feelings. With each of you speaking through a hand puppet character, can you help him with the challenges of meeting a new friend, going to the doctor, feeling sad or coping with the arrival of a new sibling? Best of all, puppets foster creativity and invite silly play, too.

• **MARBLE DROP** Save those empty bulb-shaped vinegar bottles and collect a few marbles. Remove the plastic insert from the bottle and drop the marbles one by one through the neck to hear the "clink." Pour the marbles out into a container and begin again. Sounds simple, but preschoolers find it fascinating.

Safety Reminder: This marble activity is for the preschooler who understands that marbles do not go into the mouth and that a glass bottle is fragile.

• **BUBBLEWRAP POPPING** Tape sheets of bubblewrap to your floor (large bubbles work best). Encourage your peppy grandchild to pop the bubbles. Will he jump, stamp, sit, or roll on it to hear that satisfying "pop, pop, pop"?

• **PAPER BALLS** Wad up newspaper into balls about baseball size. Secure with a little tape if necessary. A wastebasket or laundry basket makes a perfect target, and the lightweight balls will not hurt people or damage furniture.

....

OOPS! Newsprint on little fingers can leave fingerprints on your wall. If that is a concern, wrap the balls in plastic wrap.

....

• **SNOWBALLS ANY TIME** This takes a little planning and preparation but is well worth the effort. You will need some old white knee-high nylons, polyester batting, plastic wrap and dried beans or rice. Wrap a couple of tablespoons of rice in the plastic; then mold some batting around the rice packet into the shape of a ball; stuff the ball into the toe of the knee-high and tie off with a knot. Cut off the extra and use for the next ball. With lots of these ready, you can have a great snowball fight indoors...no mittens needed.

• **TOILET PAPER DECOR** Give your grandchild a full roll of toilet paper and let him decorate himself, you and the house. You may need to get it started by creating a lovely toilet paper belt or by using it to wrap the leg of the table, but soon he will get the idea. The rule of course—he must help you pick it all up later.

• **ALL ABOARD** No need to go out for a train or bus ride; just line up a few chairs, one behind the other, and you are on your way. Passengers can be animal or doll friends, and the destinations are unlimited. This activity can be even more fun if you prepare tickets, a lunch to eat on the journey, a special traveling costume or a purse full of money to take along with you.

• **SAVE USED GADGETS** An old cell phone or typewriter can be reused by your preschooler grandchild. He will have fun pretending to make calls or typing a letter. Can he find the letters that spell his name?

• PUT TOGETHER AN OFFICE KIT Gather paper punches, pens, calculators and pads of paper. With a small table as a desk, your preschooler will get right to work.

• USE A MAGNIFYING GLASS Send your grandchild on an "up close and personal" investigation of the house. Everyday things become fascinating—the pattern of the wallpaper, the fibers of the rug and the cat if she will sit still.

• DRAW A SIMPLE MAP Some rooms of your house can be mapped out. Follow the map together and check off key items as they are located (the red couch, the little stool, the dog's dish). Expand this to other rooms and even outside.

• WHERE DO YOU KEEP LOOSE CHANGE? Let your grandchild help you sort the coins. For a game, hide some pennies in a room or two and let him go on a hunt. Many charities collect pennies so this is a chance to wrap pennies and donate to the Ronald McDonald House or the Salvation Army to help others.

In the bedroom, hall or bath

• GATHER YOUR FLASHLIGHTS AND DARKEN THE ROOM for a low-tech light show. See if your grandchild can find various targets with the beam. Lie on your backs and "dance" the light on the ceiling. Can his beam catch up with yours?

• OPEN A SHOE STORE if you do not mind ending up with your shoes in a temporary jumble. With your closet as the store, your grandchild can be the salesperson and you the customer. Request a particular pair of shoes, try them on, pretend to pay—play it to the hilt with a shoe store sign, a mirror and fake money!

• PLAY DRESS UP Search your drawers and closets for items to stock a costume box knowing that most preschoolers like to dress up as pirates, superheroes, princesses or firemen. Fill it with scarves, hats, purses, ties, shoes, belts and, of course, old jewelry. The secondhand store has great possibilities for recycled party dresses and Halloween costumes. Why don't you dress up, too? Maybe the two of you can walk the runway for Grandpa.

GOING OUTSIDE

With a preschooler's eagerness to explore and understand the world around her, the outdoors is an ideal place to nurture and feed her curiosity. Many of the suggestions listed in the toddler section for outdoor play are also appropriate for a preschooler. She will enjoy the same activities, but probably for a longer period of time and at a higher developmental level. In addition, she will have many good ideas of her own...just wait and see.

 • A PRESCHOOLER IS A CRITTER LOVER She likes to explore and discover who lives outside...ants, ladybugs, sow bugs (roly-polies), caterpillars and colorful butterflies. Be her audience. Let her tell you about each bug discovery—what it is, where it lives and where it is going.

• WHAT'S HIDING IN THOSE BUSHES? If you spread an old, light-colored pillowcase under a bush and shake the branches, you might find critters you did not expect. For a closer look, use a magnifying glass. Capture them in one of those little mesh bug houses to keep for a while before shaking them back on the bush.

• DIG FOR EARTHWORMS Some children will want to hold them, while others will prefer just to watch. Place a few worms on a white sheet of paper and observe their trail of dirt. Preschoolers love to hear about the earthworm's job to munch, munch, munch and poop, poop, poop—that is how they help the garden. Carefully return the worms to their garden home when you are done, teaching by example your respect for nature and all its creatures, even the slimy and small.

• HUNT FOR LADYBUGS Remember the fun of finding them in your garden? Let the ladybug tickle her way up your preschooler's arm, and together you can make a wish before she takes off. "Ladybug, ladybug, fly away home." You can purchase ladybugs at your nursery so your grandchild can set a cloud of them free in your yard. Will they be there the next time she visits?

• SHARE OUTDOOR TASKS Preschoolers do not consider raking and watering to be work; it is play for them. Give her a child-sized shovel, broom or watering can to help shovel snow, sweep the walk or water plants.

- **GARDEN IN A POT OR TWO** If space is limited, plant one with vegetables and one with flowers. Onion sets, radishes and petunias sprout quickly.

> **Jan:** Since three of my granddaughters live far away and usually visit in the summer, I need to get the garden started before they come. It's fun for them to harvest the vegetables that I planted months before, such as carrots, tomatoes and turnips. We also plant seeds and bedding plants to tend while they're visiting that I will enjoy after they are gone.

- **MAKE THINGS OUT OF SUMMERTIME FLOWERS** Remember hollyhock dolls, daisy and clover chains, talking snapdragons and buttercups under the chin? Pass these simple, old-fashioned pleasures along to your grandchild.

- **PUMPKIN SEEDS** Planted in June, your seeds might just produce the perfect Halloween jack-o'-lantern in October.

- **CHILDREN LOVE TO DIG** for the sake of digging—in the sand, in the dirt, in the mud. Set aside a digging spot to build tunnels, scoop holes and make mud pies. They will bury and re-bury small toys, rocks and sticks.

> **Lynne:** My grandson was an avid digger and sometimes ended up covered with mud, especially when I let him use the hose to loosen the dirt. To maximize fun and minimize clean up, I kept a set of his old clothes and sandals at our house ready for messy outdoor play.

- **HELP THE SPRING BIRDS** Have your grandchild set out strands of yarn, thread and puffs of cotton or dryer lint on low bushes. Chances are they will disappear quickly as the birds gather their nest building materials. Wouldn't it be fun to find that empty nest in the fall?

- **BUILD FAIRY HOUSES** Use little twigs, nutshell halves, stones and large leaves. Draw a face on an acorn, cork or rock to put in the fairy house. Your grandchild's imagination will do the rest. Some grammies make secret visits to the fairy house to leave a tiny gift from the fairy for their grandchild to discover later.

• THE SECRET TRAIL Does your grandchild know the story of Hansel and Gretel? Rose petals from fading blossoms make ideal "crumbs" for your grandchild to drop on her way to a hiding spot. Once she is ready to be found, follow her trail and find her before she bursts with excitement.

• HUNT FOR STONES AND PEBBLES Your grandchild may want to sort them by size and color or show you how many she can count. Choose some smooth, fist-sized stones to wash off and paint or decorate with magic markers and glitter. They can dress up your garden or be a special gift.

 Laurie: Stones in my grandson's hands were potential missiles, so we set aside an "OK zone" for throwing in our yard. Adding a target made it even more fun.

Some activities require a bit of preparation

• DIG FOR DINOSAUR BONES Collect well-scrubbed good-sized bones (turkey carcass, steak, chop and large soup bones) until you have an assortment to bury. Some butchers will donate to your cause if you make a request. Boil washed bones for 30 minutes in a 2:1 solution of water to vinegar; dry them and bake at low heat for an hour to assure odor-free storage until the hunt. Hide the bones in a sandbox or garden area for your young archeologist to discover. She can arrange them later on paper and name her new dinosaur species.

• HUNT FOR GOLD To hunt for pirate's gold or the "pot o' gold" on St. Patrick's Day, spray small stones with metallic gold or silver paint. Let them dry and then hide them in sand, under bushes, in nooks and crannies all about. Offer your grandchild a loot bag as she sets off to hunt.

• BUILD YOUR OWN VOLCANO No need to buy a kit—you probably have everything on hand. With your grandchild, mound sand, dirt or mulch into a "mountain" and insert a small paper cup in the top. She can fill the cup halfway with baking soda and pour a half-cup or so of vinegar slowly into the paper cup. Get ready for the eruption as the bubbles overflow the cup. For an even more authentic lava flow, add red food coloring to the vinegar. (Be prepared with an entire box of baking soda and a bottle of vinegar, as one volcano is NEVER enough!) Your grandchild may stick twig "trees" in the path of the flow or even want to add small animals, cars or leaf homes to the scene.

• **TRICK THE FLOWERS** Are there calla lilies or white daisies or white carnations growing in your yard? Cut two or three of these long-stemmed beauties and set up an experiment. Put the flowers in a clear jar or vase, pour in a cup of water, and let your grandchild add eight drops of food coloring. Check the flowers in three or four hours and see how the white blossoms have changed color.

• **PLANT A GARDEN TOGETHER** Choose flowers, vegetables or bulbs that you know will grow well in your area. Seeds that grow easily and quickly are sunflowers, peppers, sweet peas and beans. To get a head start on your harvest, consider buying bedding plants. Show your grandchild how to dig a hole, loosen the roots on plants and pat dirt around the seedlings. What else is needed? Just bit of water, the warm sun and lots of patience. Here is a chance to encourage self-sustaining farming!

• **NEED A SCARECROW?** Stuff some outgrown clothes or Grandpa's old shirt and jeans with rags or straw. Add a head made of a stuffed pillowcase (your grandchild could draw the face with a permanent marker), top it with a straw hat, and then seat it on a bench or tie it to a stake or broomstick for support. Would your preschooler like to name your scarecrow and make up stories about him?

• **PLAY WITH WATER** Provide a shallow tub of water (perhaps an old dishpan) and add some boats, funnels, turkey basters and cups. If you have two clear plastic containers, fill them with water and use food coloring to tint one blue and the other yellow. Inevitably your grandchild will mix the two and surprise herself with a new color. Adult supervision is always required when children are near water.

OOPS! Hands may also get slightly colored and require a few washings with soap to remove the stains.

- **SET UP AN OBSTACLE COURSE** Practice walking, running or hopping over, under, around and through it. You can use outdoor furniture, coiled or uncoiled hoses, planters or whatever the two of you find to make the route more interesting.

Weather or not...

- **IS IT RAINING TODAY?** Put on raincoats and boots to go for a rain walk. Note the smells and sounds. Where are the birds today? Perhaps you can find a small stream of water in the yard or along a sidewalk to dam up with pebbles or to float a leaf or twig boat.

- **WATCH THE CLOUDS** Imagine what shapes they make on a windy day.

- **TRY CATCHING THE WIND** Shake open a large plastic trash bag and give one side of the open end to your grandchild while you hold the other. Run together into the wind, the bag will fill, and you have trapped Mr. Wind. If you tie it tightly closed, Mr. Wind cannot escape.

 *Lynne:* I still smile remembering when my grandson caught Mr. Wind and insisted we take him inside and show Grandpa. Luckily Grandpa played along and talked through the bag to Mr. Wind. Then together they gently opened the bag and let Mr. Wind go.

- **KITES ARE GREAT PLAYMATES** and can be made simply:

    - Cut strips from plastic trash bags. Tuck them in your pocket or purse to whip out when that perfect gust comes along.

    - Use plastic bags with handles. Tie a long string to each handle and hold the bag open so the wind can fill it...a kite flying success for even a very young child.

    - Color a paper plate. Attach plastic or crepe paper streamers to one side and a string to the other, and then run, run as fast as you can.

- **A CLEAR NIGHT IS FOR INVESTIGATING THE WONDERS IN THE SKY** Can you find the man in the moon? Point out constellations that are easily recognizable. Toilet paper tubes used as binoculars can help focus the gaze of your mini-astronomer.

When it snows

• BUILD SMALL VILLAGES in snowdrifts for plastic animals or figures. How about using those summer sand toys and trucks and diggers in the winter snow?

• PLAY DETECTIVE As you walk in the snow, whose tracks or footprints do you recognize? Could it be a rabbit, the family dog, a deer, bird, mouse or squirrel?

• ROLL SNOWBALLS Stacked snowballs can become a fort or snow wall.

 TIP: Do not forget to use sunscreen. Sun reflected off the snow can be surprisingly intense.

• SELECT A TARGET Snowball throwing is more fun with a target, such as a tree or bush. See how close your preschooler can come to the bullseye.

• BUILD A SNOWMAN Encourage your preschooler to dress him with personality. Is he a classic Frosty, a family member or a storybook character?

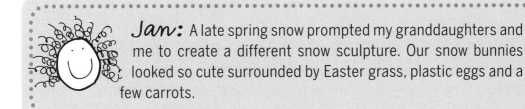

Jan: A late spring snow prompted my granddaughters and me to create a different snow sculpture. Our snow bunnies looked so cute surrounded by Easter grass, plastic eggs and a few carrots.

• FAIRIES NEED A SNOWMAN Make a tiny snowman with a bottle-cap hat and some yarn for a scarf as the finishing touches.

• DIG SNOW TUNNELS OR CAVES This will take a lot of energy after a big snowfall.

• GO SLEDDING Remember that plastic bags, cardboard and inner tubes can be sleds, too.

• TRY ICE SKATING No need for skates...boots can provide lots of slippery fun on ice.

• REMEMBER PLAYING THE GAME FOX AND GEESE? Tramp a circle in the snow with two paths crossing in the center like an X. One of you plays the fox and chases the other(s) while all have to stay on the trampled path. Little legs move fast...your grandchild can catch you in this simple chase game.

The great outdoors is filled with endless possibilities for exploration and discovery. Biologist and author, Rachel Carson, underscored how important it is for a child to have a special adult in her life to share her sense of wonder. You can be that unhurried companion reinforcing her learning about Mother Nature's creatures and her respect for the environment.

THE NEIGHBORHOOD AND BEYOND

For successful outings with your grandchild, remember these three cardinal rules:

- Consider the child's age and interests.

- Take into account energy and stamina levels...both his and yours.

- Be flexible. If an outing is not going well, head for home and try it another day.

The circus is coming to town! Remember the excitement of seeing acrobats, clowns and trained animals under the Big Top? It might be a treat for your grandchild...or maybe not. Some preschoolers have the attention span to sit through a long show. Others could be frustrated trying to stay seated while the action is too far away for him to feel involved. Most preschoolers prefer to be on the move and in the midst of activity.

There are lots of places the two of you can visit. Some are close to home and require only an hour or two, while others are better for a full day outing. Some are more appropriate for younger preschoolers, while others work well for mixed ages.

Quick Stops

Most communities have some kind of open space, or a park or school play yard. Bring a ball or bubble mix for the youngest child; the older ones will probably head for the play equipment. This is a good destination when amusing children of different ages.

• **STOP AT A GROCERY STORE** Your grandchild can help with the shopping. Could he choose some fruit or yogurt for lunch, count out the carrots you need or perhaps select tomorrow's breakfast cereal? Some stores have those cute shopping baskets for children to push by themselves or shopping carts that have a mini-car built in the front. A "road trip" down the grocery aisle in one of those cars is such fun, as you tell your grandchild to "turn right at the bananas" or "stop at the milk on the left."

• **HEAD FOR THE BAKERY DEPARTMENT** Your grocery store bakery can be a fascinating place to watch as cakes are frosted or donuts are being pulled from the oven. The baker may offer a free treat just for saying "please."

• IS THERE A CONSTRUCTION SITE NEARBY? Grandsons will especially love this. Stop to watch the graders, rollers, steam shovels, cranes and dump trucks.

Laurie: It's amazing what children learn when their interest is high. My grandson was still struggling with basic vocabulary words, but he could name many different pieces of construction equipment when we watched a home being built in our neighborhood. He knew the difference between an excavator and a front loader. I had to look it up!

• GOT A LETTER TO MAIL? A trip to the Post Office can spark a wonderful conversation about how letters travel from here to their destination. Could your grandchild make a card and mail it to himself?

• VISIT YOUR LOCAL FIRE DEPARTMENT Check ahead to see if they allow visitors. Rare is the firefighter who does not welcome the chance to show off the shiny engines, talk about fire safety or demonstrate the Stop, Drop and Roll technique.

• CALL YOUR LOCAL LIBRARY Find out when there is a preschool story time. After story hour you can browse, read together and check out some books to take home.

• GO TO A PET STORE This can be a rainy day destination to discover all its fuzzy, furry and feathered friends. You might make the trip a search for specific information: look for the different kinds of food animals eat or see how many animal homes your grandchild can identify.

Cindy: Our community had an art gallery featuring photographs of wildlife. My grandchildren were fascinated with the pictures and, on a rainy day, visiting it was almost as good as going to the zoo.

Climb aboard

• TAKE A RIDE ON A LOCAL BUS   Your preschooler may want to hand the money to the driver. Let him point out what he sees out the window and ring the bell when it is time to get off.

• HIS FIRST TRAIN RIDE You could be the one to introduce your grandchild to real trains. Make every aspect exciting—buying the tickets, waiting on the platform, climbing aboard, watching scenery speed by and getting off at the right stop. Plan a short ride for his first trip, perhaps stopping at a park and returning on the train after play and a picnic.

Splish splash

Safety Reminder: Preschoolers can better understand water dangers and may not need the physical restraint they did when they were younger but, that said, they still need constant supervision. When near any body of water, remember the AAP's Touch Rule: Near or in water, keep your child close enough to touch.

Is there a pond, lake or stream nearby?

• ARE THERE TADPOLES OR MINNOWS swimming near shore? If it is permitted to throw small bits of bread in the water, you may attract a school of fish or some ducklings.

• LOOK FOR A FROG SUNNING HIMSELF on a nearby lily pad. See how fast he jumps into the water if he's startled! Can your grandchild leap like a frog?

• SAIL A LEAF BOAT Put a leaf in the moving water of a stream and watch it float away. You could have Grammie and Me boat races. How far do you think our boats can go...to a lake, a river or even the ocean?

• THROW PEBBLES INTO THE WATER one by one. Look both ways to be certain that no one is in the way. Watch the ripples grow when the pebble hits the water. Can you show him how to "skip" a stone?

• GO FISHING   Does your older preschooler have enough patience to wait for a nibble? All he needs is a pole, line, hook and a wad of bread for bait. Pretending to fish can also be fun. Tie a string on a stick, and fasten a cork at the end of the string.

Cindy: For my grandsons, the best part of fishing was the "bait hunt" the night before. Armed with a flashlight and a jar for collecting, we looked for night crawlers in the grass. Although our purpose was to catch those wiggly worms, I suspect the real treat was just being outside in the dark.

Excursions

• TAKE A DRIVE through the countryside and stop for a picnic in the shade of a big tree. Do you see any squirrels looking for nuts, horses running in the fields, cows grazing on the hillside or ants heading for your juice box? Pull out your smart phone for a picture of the scene...it will help him tell the story to Grandpa later.

Jan: Planned outings sometimes go awry. I couldn't wait to take my grandchildren to see the Great Oak–a huge oak tree with arched branches reaching the ground. But alas, while trudging through the field to get there, stickers stuck to their little socks while scratchy branches and uneven ground made walking difficult. "What's so great about a great oak anyway?" I heard them grumble. They definitely remember the hike to the Great Oak—but not as I hoped. I will try again when they're older.

• VISIT A FOREST PRESERVE and take a short hike in the woods. Who is hiding there—squirrels, bunnies or slugs? Who can you hear but not see—insects, birds or snakes? Who lives in the hole in the ground or up in that nest? If you are lucky, maybe you will see a deer.

• HEAD FOR THE BEACH Build sand castles, hunt for seashells or play in the waves. Take along a kite if it is breezy.

....

 TIP: For full day adventures, it pays to be prepared. Take along emergency numbers and your cell phone; pack sunscreen, drinks, snacks and extra diapers if needed. Tuck a packet of wipes in your purse to clean up those little hands before snacks or a lunch break. Finally, it never hurts to have a change of clothes for your preschooler...you just never know.

....

Community attractions

• GO TO CLASSES FOR PRESCHOOLERS You may be able to attend a gym, dance or music class, Mommy and Me or sports session with him on a one-time trial basis.

• WATCH FOR SPECIAL EVENTS Puppet shows or fairs are examples that may be appropriate for your preschooler. Some areas have children's theater groups where youthful actors and actresses perform plays for young audiences. Check out your local newspaper or search the web for "children's activities" followed by your city's name.

Cindy: One of our favorite autumn outings was going to the pumpkin patch where each grandchild chose his own pumpkin. I learned after the first year to limit the size to what each child could carry by himself. Otherwise, they always went for the biggest one. We saved that honor for Grandpa.

• ANY SPORTING EVENT NEARBY? Maybe you and Grandpa can take your grandchild to a ball game. Try a high school or local college game first to see how it goes. If that is a success, he may be ready to take in a professional game, a bigger investment in time and money. Some preschoolers may not make it through the entire game the first few times.

• VISIT THE ZOO Preschoolers love it...from the noisy monkeys and the huge elephants, to the otters and snakes. In the spring, you might even see some baby animals. Plan your itinerary before you go to make sure you see the animals your grandchild is most interested in. It can be followed up with a picnic or a quick lunch.

 TIP: A petting zoo is a good first step for some children. It is an opportunity to observe, pet, feed and get to know domesticated animals. Smaller animals in close proximity are more approachable and less intimidating.

• LOOK FOR CHILDREN'S MUSEUMS with areas designed to appeal to preschoolers. Remember when we could only stand and look through the glass at displays? Today's children experience exhibits in a multi-sensory way. They can hold a hermit crab at the indoor tide pool or see if they can identify animal sounds from recordings...clear examples of the hands-on, interactive approach to early learning endorsed by educators today.

Movin' on

These so-called Magic Years of preschool are ending. Your five-year-old grandchild will soon be heading off to kindergarten, with new challenges and the experiences of "real" school. Are your special moments over with this fledgling? Not on your life! He will always need special grammie time— your focused interest, your one-on-one involvement and unconditional love.

May the magic continue...

CHAPTER 5

MUSIC FROM HEAD TO TOE

AHH MUSIC...REMEMBER THE PLEASURE IT GAVE YOUR CHILDREN when they were young? It is the same for little ones today. The nursery rhymes, sing-along songs and lullabies of years ago continue to be favorites. What is new is our more complete understanding of the benefits music brings to the very young child.

Active involvement is the key here just as it is with child's play. We now know that as a child enjoys music from head to toe by wiggling her body to the beat or singing at top volume, she is at the same time stimulating the motor and cognitive areas of her brain. These types of experiences with music help prepare her for the reading and math skills she will need later in school.

The good news, Grammie, is that you can be instrumental in promoting such benefits. Best of all, you will have fun doing it!

Need to refresh your memory of songs young children enjoy? Lyrics to many traditional songs and finger plays are in the Appendix in alphabetical order by title; your favorites are probably among them. For the complete verses of these and more children's songs, check with your local music store or go to http://kids.niehs.nih.gov/games/songs.

MUSIC AND RHYMES FOR INFANTS

Singing and rhyming are some of the best ways to "talk" with infants as well as entertain them. They love hearing a familiar voice croon or speak softly. By simply doing what comes naturally as you cradle and rock your grandchild, did you realize you are helping his brain develop? The repetitive sounds and rhythms stimulate his speech and language growth.

First songs and soothers

Every infant needs a little soothing now and then. Humming lullabies while rubbing a sleepy infant's back or rocking him before naptime can be calming.

- **Rock-a-bye Baby:** The perfect rocking chair lullaby.

Laurie: The original version of *Rock-a-bye Baby* ended with the baby and cradle in a heap on the ground. My granddaughter learned my gentler version: "Rock-a-bye baby in the treetop. When the wind blows, the cradle will rock. When the bough bends, we'll all take a peek to see if the baby is fast asleep."

- **Twinkle, Twinkle, Little Star:** The age-old nighttime song for lulling Baby to sleep.

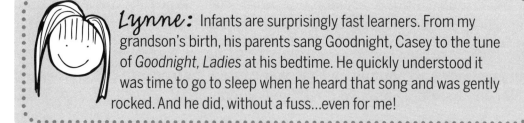

Lynne: Infants are surprisingly fast learners. From my grandson's birth, his parents sang Goodnight, Casey to the tune of *Goodnight, Ladies* at his bedtime. He quickly understood it was time to go to sleep when he heard that song and was gently rocked. And he did, without a fuss...even for me!

To amuse your grandchild and maybe bring a chuckle, try these:

• **Pat-A-Cake:** Likely the first game played with an infant because the hand motions can be used with even a newborn.

WORDS	ACTIONS
Pat-a-cake, pat-a-cake, baker's man, *Bake me a cake as fast as you can.*	Gently clap baby's hands together in rhythm.
Roll it,	Move baby's hands in a circular motion around each other.
And pat it,	Tap palm with one finger.
And mark it with a B,	Trace the letter B on baby's palm.
And toss it in the oven for (Baby's name) and me.	Raise both hands high above baby's head.

• **This Little Piggy:** The classic excuse for wiggling those cute little toes.

• **Mousie:** Fingers scamper up toward Baby's chin.

• **Hickory Dickory Dock:** This chant brings giggles as you tickle Baby's arm.

• **Mary Had a Little Lamb:** A simple song that's easy to sing because there is so much repetition.

• **Trot, Trot to Boston:** A horsey ride on Grammie's knee with a surprise ending.

WORDS	ACTIONS
Trot, trot to Boston, *Trot, trot to Lynn.*	Bounce baby gently as he sits on your knees.
Look out little boy (girl), *Or you'll fall in!*	Hold baby firmly, as you suddenly part your knees, and allow baby to "fall" between your legs.

And, of course, there is always "Dancing with the Stars"...Grammie-style. Turn on your favorite music—anything from rap to classical. Scoop up Baby and twirl away. He will enjoy the rhythmic movement and you will get some exercise.

MUSIC FOR TODDLERS

Most toddlers hear a catchy tune and respond spontaneously. They cannot resist—they bounce their bodies and nod their heads. Take advantage of their need to "get physical" and as often as you can, join your grandchild marching, clapping and moving to the beat. It is good for both of you.

OOPS! A few children have a low tolerance for anything loud, including music. Others go for more volume. Start low and turn up the sound slowly until both you and your toddler are happy with it.

Remember how children naturally love to mimic? Toddlers are old enough to learn the words to songs or copy the actions of finger plays. With their improving coordination and language ability, they will surprise you with their eagerness to perform.

Lynne: I often phoned my sister so she could hear my eighteen-month-old grandson sing. She was an enthusiastic listener and he nearly burst with pride hearing her cheers. He realized something new and exciting—he had a skill that others could appreciate. What a boost to his developing sense of self!

Movin' along with music

Toddlers sing purely for joy. Teach your grandchild one of your own favorite songs, add some hand motions that she can imitate, and you are on your way to fun together.

Here is a list of Top Tunes for Toddlers, beginning with the simplest tunes that are easy for young children to master.

• ***ABC Song:*** To the same melody as *Twinkle, Twinkle, Little Star.*

• ***Happy Birthday:*** Fun to sing any time...birthday or not.

• ***Jingle Bells:*** Popular all year round. Even more fun with shakers or bells.

• **Old MacDonald Had a Farm:** This sing-along song gives toddlers a chance to hear the stanzas and join in the refrain. Ask your grandchild to choose the animal and make its sound. Roaring lions? Just for fun, pretend they live on the farm, too!

Lynne: I always sang to my young grandchildren but didn't realize they were paying attention. Imagine my surprise when, at only one year, one of my grandsons added "E-I-E-I-O" all by himself to *Old MacDonald Had a Farm.* Maybe singing runs in the family.

• **Where is Thumbkin?:** An easy action song that enhances coordination.

• **Eensy, Weensy Spider:** Children love to mimic the spider going up and the rain coming down.

• **If You're Happy and You Know It:** A good song for expressing feelings.

• **Wheels on the Bus:** Doors, windshield wipers, horns and people all move on this bus.

• **Row, Row, Row Your Boat:** Sing and row the boat with your grandchild partner.

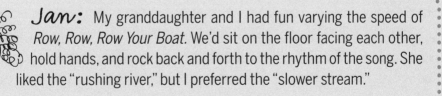

Jan: My granddaughter and I had fun varying the speed of *Row, Row, Row Your Boat.* We'd sit on the floor facing each other, hold hands, and rock back and forth to the rhythm of the song. She liked the "rushing river," but I preferred the "slower stream."

• **Pop Goes the Weasel:** Children cannot wait until it is time to pop up.

• **I'm a Little Teapot:** Following Grammie's lead, a toddler uses her arms as the handle and spout as she pretends to be a teapot.

Finger plays

Waiting for those cookies to bake? Have a few minutes before Grandpa gets home or Mommy arrives? That is the perfect time for a finger play or two.

• ***Open, Shut Them:*** Easy for even a one-year-old to follow.

• ***Two Little Blackbirds:*** Simple to learn and perform using only "pointer" fingers.

• ***Five Little Monkeys:*** Toddlers quickly identify with these "naughty" monkeys who love jumping on the bed.

• ***Birthday Finger Play:*** Toddlers love to make and bake a pretend birthday cake.

• ***Here is a Bunny:*** A toddler's fingers make funny ears for the bunny who dives into a hole.

• ***Here is the Church:*** Tricky for toddlers to do on their own but they will be entertained by your demonstration.

MUSIC FOR PRESCHOOLERS

By the time a child is three, he probably has his own favorite songs. Developmentally he is now more able to keep rhythms, remember the words and stay on tune. Listen to him sing the *ABC Song*…all by himself, no prompting needed.

Here is a reminder list of some classics for this age. Try them out as you are taking a walk with your grandchild, pushing him on a swing or filling some down time. No doubt you will remember others you sang as a child or with your own children. Do not be shy or think you have to be an opera star—your grandchild does not love you for your pitch-perfect voice, so belt it out!

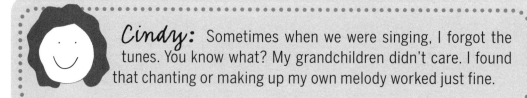

Cindy: Sometimes when we were singing, I forgot the tunes. You know what? My grandchildren didn't care. I found that chanting or making up my own melody worked just fine.

Sing-along songs

• **Are You Sleeping?:** The English version of *Frère Jacques*. Will the morning bells wake him up?

• **Down by the Station:** Does your grandchild know what a puffer belly is? Train-loving preschoolers do!

• **I've Been Working on the Railroad:** Lots of verses for hiking or riding in the car.

 Laurie: We used to sing *She'll Be Coming 'Round the Mountain* as a family on road trips. The possibilities for verses were limited only by our stamina!

• **John Jacob Jingleheimer Schmidt:** Preschoolers are proud when they can finally sing this fellow's name. As you sing, get progressively quieter with each verse. Your grandchild's job is to shout out the Da-da's in the chorus as loud as he can.

• **Polly Put the Kettle On:** Goes perfectly with a tea party.

• **This Old Man:** Great for counting, silly rhyming and knick-knack paddy-whacking.

• **Yankee Doodle:** Pasta-loving preschoolers always giggle at the word macaroni. Did you know this song is over 250 years old?

• **You are My Sunshine:** A bright and cheery song for a cloudy day.

 Laurie: Who knows how or why a child chooses his personal favorite song? Because it was one his father always requested, I taught that sunshine song to my grandson at an early age. He loved it, too, and for years it was the one we always sang first and last.

• **Zip-a-dee-doo-dah:** An upbeat song for that wonderful feeling when you head outdoors on a sunny day.

Mother Goose rhymes

Mother Goose poems have been popular for centuries and tell stories that are part of our culture. Sing and chant them with your preschooler, building vocabulary and rhyming skills along the way.

• *Baa, Baa, Black Sheep:* Does your grandchild know where wool comes from?

• *Humpty Dumpty:* Some things cannot be fixed even by the king's men.

• *Jack and Jill:* A classic nursery rhyme that is easy to sing and act out.

• *Jack Be Nimble:* Can your grandchild pretend to jump over the candlestick?

• *Little Boy Blue:* A haystack…what a place to fall asleep!

• *Little Miss Muffett:* Your preschooler can sit on a footstool or a stack of pillows and act this song out.

Get them up and going

Songs can lift a child's sagging spirits. To make him laugh, simply change key words like this: "the eensy, weensy 'elephant' went up the kitchen wall." You can also use songs to make routine tasks more fun. Improvise with words that fit the situation or capture his attention by putting his name into the lyrics. These are real tricks of the trade.

• *Lazy Mary:* Will your grandchild ever get out of bed? Use her name in place of Mary.

• *Heigh-Ho, Heigh-Ho:* Off to play, off to bed, off to the car…adapt this song to wherever you are both going.

• *Mary Had a Little Lamb:* Useful melody for singing your way through the routines of the day with your grandchild. For example, "Now it's time to drink your milk, drink your milk, drink your milk. Now it's time to drink your milk. It makes you big and strong."

- **When the Saints Go Marching In:** A peppy song to accompany many activities.

> *Oh, when (child's name) goes marching in ...*
>
> *Oh, when it's time to sit and eat...*
>
> *Oh, let's begin to pick up toys...*

- **Here We Go 'Round the Mulberry Bush:** Daily grooming made easy.

> *This is the way we brush our teeth,*
>
> > *brush our teeth, brush our teeth,*
>
> *This is the way we brush our teeth, so early in the morning.*
>
> *This is the way we comb our hair...*
>
> *This is the way we put on our shirt...*

- **The Bear Went Over the Mountain:** A good transitional song when there is a hill to climb or a need to shift activities.

> *My face is ready for washing...*
>
> *My feet are ready for walking...*
>
> *My books are ready for reading...*

- **The Farmer in the Dell:** Distract a child at a stubborn moment or ease him into tasks like cleaning up toys or getting buckled into that car seat.

> *It's time to eat our lunch,*
>
> *So let's go wash our hands,*
>
> *Hi-Ho, the derry-o,*
>
> *It's time to wash and eat.*

Want more of a workout?

These popular tunes have actions that most preschoolers eagerly try to master. Some would be especially fun at a party or a family gathering.

• *Head and Shoulders, Knees and Toes:* Sing to the tune of *There Is a Tavern in the Town.*

WORDS	ACTIONS
Head and shoulders, knees and toes, knees and toes,	Touch or point to each body part as you sing.
Head and shoulders, knees and toes, knees and toes,	Sing slowly at first, then faster and faster with each verse.
And eyes and ears and mouth and nose.	
Head and shoulders, knees and toes, knees and toes.	

• *The Grand Old Duke of York:* A real grammie knee workout as you show your preschooler how to do the "ups," the "downs" and the "half ways."

• *One, Two, Buckle My Shoe:* A peppy rhyme that reinforces counting.

• *Skip, Skip, Skip to My Lou:* Good for preschoolers learning to skip.

• *The Ants Go Marching:* One-by-one, two-by-two, a catchy tune to liven up the mood and motivate a hiker.

• *Hokey Pokey:* Be creative. There is no "right" way to do the hokey-pokey but it is always fun.

• *London Bridge:* Can you and Grandpa capture that little one when the bridge comes falling down?

• *Ring Around the Rosie:* A circle game for two or more where everyone falls down and then jumps back up.

• *A Tisket, A Tasket:* Best sung with at least five children and props of a basket and envelope.

MUSIC FOR ALL AGES

Listening

There is a time and place for just listening to music…perhaps when your grandchild is resting on your lap, riding in the car or you are working on an art project together. Expose her to a broad spectrum of music, both instrumental and vocal. Why not expand her musical palate and introduce her to some of your own favorites? It is important for children to see that adults, too, enjoy music.

• DIG OUT YOUR OLD RECORD PLAYER if you have held on to it all these years and play one of your favorite 78s or 45s. In addition to the songs, your grandchild will likely be entertained by the mechanics of the phonograph and ask where you got those "giant CDs."

....

 TIP: Little people have big ears. We used to know what our children were listening to because with phonographs and radios we could hear the music, too. However with today's individual listening devices, parents and grandparents need to be aware that children might hear lyrics not meant for young ears. Either be sure that what is recorded is appropriate for young ones or keep the music player out of reach.

....

OOPS! Young children think ear buds are cool. If they use them, set the volume at a low level to protect against hearing loss.

 Laurie: Whenever my two-year-old grandson and I were on the road together, we entertained ourselves singing some songs we both knew. This was fine for short jaunts or until we ran out of ideas. For longer journeys, we sang, often quite loudly, to the music of children's CDs. We were our own best audience!

Dancing

Young children freely interpret the mood of the music. They march to the sound of a band, sway to a more lyrical symphonic sound and romp and stomp to a country beat.

 **Lynne:** One of my three-year-old grandson's favorite toys was his little portable keyboard. He'd press the keys for the rhythms or tunes he wanted, and then dance and clap to the music. He was feeling the music, rocking and rolling from his toes to his curly blond hair!

• FOLLOW THE LEADER Turn on the music and move to the beat. Can she imitate you? Now let her lead and you follow.

• MIRROR DANCE Turn on the music and let your grandchild dance in front of a full-length mirror to enjoy her own performance.

• GOT A STASH OF SILKY SCARVES? Bring them out. They add flair to any musical performance. Wave them as you dance together or wad one into a ball, toss it in the air and watch your grandchild try to catch it.

Making music

• INVERTED POTS AND PANS, BOXES, OATMEAL CARTONS and coffee cans become noisy drums.

• PLASTIC EGGS OR FROZEN JUICE CANS FILLED WITH BEANS, rice or small pebbles and taped securely shut, become shakers.

• PAPER TOWEL OR TOILET PAPER TUBES are horns for a parade.

• RUBBER BANDS OF DIFFERENT SIZES stretched over a shoebox or tissue box make a stringed guitar.

 • INEXPENSIVE, DURABLE, CHILD-SIZED INSTRUMENTS are available in catalogs, children's toy stores and on the internet. Some come in sets that contain shakers, bells, cymbals and triangles and are good choices for all ages. Depending on their skill level, children use the instruments to make their own music or accompany music they are listening to.

• XYLOPHONES are a step beyond simple percussive instruments. A child can make and listen to accurate musical tones—higher and lower, louder and softer. She will learn to tap out favorite tunes in no time.

The real thing

Do not pass up a chance to expose your grandchild to live music. Whether in your own living room or in a concert hall, the experience gives her the opportunity to not only see the actual instruments but also hear the rich sounds they make.

• WITH A PIANO OR KEYBOARD, help your grandchild discover how the low notes sound like the rumble of thunder or a lion's roar. What does she think of when she hears the tinkle of high notes—maybe a little bird or falling raindrops? Preschoolers can even learn to plunk out simple songs like *Happy Birthday.*

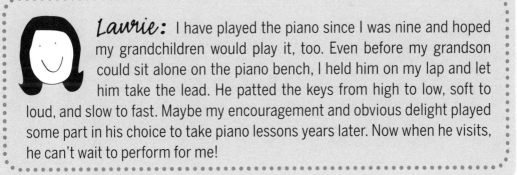

Laurie: I have played the piano since I was nine and hoped my grandchildren would play it, too. Even before my grandson could sit alone on the piano bench, I held him on my lap and let him take the lead. He patted the keys from high to low, soft to loud, and slow to fast. Maybe my encouragement and obvious delight played some part in his choice to take piano lessons years later. Now when he visits, he can't wait to perform for me!

• IF YOU PLAY AN INSTRUMENT, be sure to share it. Show him how to strum your guitar, blow on your harmonica or use the bow on your violin or cello.

• LOOK FOR CONCERTS designed just for young audiences. If you like children's songs and group participation (and you do not mind noisy fun bordering on chaos), take him to one of these events.

• HOLIDAY PERFORMANCES can be a good way to celebrate the season and introduce your grandchild to musical productions. Be forewarned: they may be rather lengthy and the audience may not appreciate a wiggly, chatty child. Listening beforehand to the music or story, however, will make it familiar and may help her stay more attentive. Be prepared to leave at intermission if necessary.

• OUTDOOR MUSICAL EVENTS are a good choice for this age child. She will have a place to move about when the show seems long and she gets restless.

A final word about music

There are so many ways to enjoy musical moments with your grandchild. Playfully join her as she sings, marches and claps. Be her best audience as she performs. Expose her to a variety of musical styles. However you add music to the time you spend with your grandchild, it is a happier, livelier day.

CHAPTER 6

READING:
MOTHER GOOSE AND BEYOND

"ONCE UPON A TIME" IS ONLY THE BEGINNING. Children have been entertained, educated and inspired by stories through the ages. Parents have known instinctively that reading to little ones would encourage appreciation for books and learning. So what is new? Research now supports that parental intuition. Education author Jim Trelease advocates in *The Read-Aloud Handbook* that, indeed, reading to children is the very best way to prepare them to be readers. Learning to relax and settle down quietly with a story also strengthens concentration skills which are helpful for success later in school.

This is where a grammie comes in. You may have more time to read to your grandchild than his parents do. Seize the opportunity whenever possible to have fun with books together…in the back seat of the car, on a park bench, in a doctor's waiting room or snuggled side-by-side on the couch. Tuck a tiny book or two into your bag when you are on the go with your grandchild so that wherever you are, you have books within reach.

The content and illustrations in children's books have changed over the years. Books published in the last decade use more innovative art techniques, deal more directly with psychological topics and offer children broader cultural exposure. The characters are certainly more diverse. Themes range from the fun and fanciful to more serious ones exploring feelings, family issues and environmental concerns.

Finding books for your grandchild

Buying a new book can be expensive, but when it is his own to keep, a child is more likely to be invested in the reading experience. Whether you buy or borrow children's books, it is important to have a variety available. Booksellers and children's librarians can be valuable resources for titles of old favorites as well as new releases. Check out your neighborhood bookstore to find what is on their shelves that your grandchild might like. Visit the children's room of your public library. Remember that garage sales or trading with friends are also ways to add to your story time book collection.

For suggestions on specific books and topics, you can also browse through guides to children's literature, such as *Valerie and Walter's Best Books for Children* by Valerie Lewis and Walter Mayes. They will help you make age-appropriate selections that fit your grandchild as he grows.

 TIP: Many library systems have a bookstore where used children's books are sold at very reduced prices. It is an inexpensive way to offer your grandchild a broad choice of reading material.

Laurie: I was so glad I saved those old encyclopedias. I pulled them out for my four-year-old granddaughter. She selected Volume C, the first letter of her name. We flipped through pages with pictures of camels, cattle, Chicago, clocks, colors, corn, cowboys and cuckoos and learned a lot!

READING WITH INFANTS

It is never too early to set up a pattern of reading with your grandchild. You can start with books like Tana Hoban's *White on Black* and Sandra Boynton's *Doggies* that can be enjoyed from birth. An older baby may grab the book, turn it upside down, flip it closed or even just chew on it…his first way to show a love of books.

Jan: I kept my camera handy because I knew that some day when they could read novels on their own, my twin grandchildren would get a kick out of seeing how they literally "devoured" their first books.

Books can be a means for a conversation-in-arms. When read to, a baby hears the rhythms and intonations of oral language, and eventually learns vocabulary. Rather than worrying about reading each and every printed word or turning the pages in order, follow Baby's lead.

Studies show that children in their first year can differentiate colors, remember phrases and connect what they see with what they hear. It may be a while before they can verbalize what you have read to them, but they begin to understand the words and overall meaning and are storing up information continually.

A baby loves repetition. Read a favorite book over and over to her. You and your grandchild can point to the pictures, exaggerate and imitate animal sounds together, or laugh at the funny faces you make in a mirror on the page. Even a ten-month-old realizes that her book about farm animals provokes your enthusiastic "Mooooo" when she turns to the cow picture. Do not hold back! Be dramatic. She will love to watch you being silly and enjoying her books as much as she does.

Here are some of our top choices for infants:

• **Ruth Bornstein, *Little Gorilla*** His jungle friends love Little Gorilla even when he is no longer tiny.

• **Sandra Boynton, *Barnyard Dance!*** A board book with bold illustrations and easy for a child to "read" on his own.

• **Margaret Wise Brown,** *Good Night Moon* A classic with a mouse hiding on each page.

• **Mem Fox,** *Time for Bed* Perfect bedtime rhyming book with beautiful pictures of animals as they curl up to go to sleep.

• **Dorothy Kunhardt,** *Pat the Bunny* Popular since 1940 with its opportunities for Baby to touch and sniff.

• **Bill Martin, Jr.,** *Brown Bear, Brown Bear, What Do You See?* One of a series of books illustrated by Eric Carle using an ask-and-respond format with colors and animal names.

• **Iona Opie, ed.,** *My Very First Mother Goose* Rosemary Wells has some surprises in her illustrations in this book of nursery rhymes.

• **Vera Williams,** *More, More, More, Said the Baby: 3 Love Stories* What baby does not want more of Mommy, Daddy and Grandma?

Board books are sturdy and often sized perfectly for little hands to hold. Soft cloth books are also favorites with infants. Some include a little fabric animal, insect or object tucked inside and attached on a cord or ribbon so it can move onto each page. Plastic books can float in the tub or be left out in the rain. If held with sticky hands, they can be wiped off with a damp cloth. All of these books are designed to be durable for this stage of reading.

Lynne: A friend who loves to sew cut squares of colorful children's fabric and stitched them together along one side to bind it like a book. Each time she and her infant granddaughter flipped through the "pages," she made up a story based on the pictures printed on the cloth—a special and personal type of reading.

Novelty books or those with special effects offer an entertainment bonus for infants. *Fuzzy Yellow Ducklings* by Matthew Van Fleet is an appealing update to the familiar touch-and-feel standard, *Pat the Bunny.* Katherine Howard's *Little Bunny Follows His Nose* invites the child to smell familiar odors as the bunny travels about. Many other books offer sound effects to listen to or mirrors to gaze in.

> **Cindy:** Sharing books with my grandson has always been part of our time together. When he was a baby, rather than drawings, he preferred actual photographs of children, food, trucks and his favorite animal, elephants. I guess, even as an infant, each child has an "eye" for what he likes.

Infants like the excitement and surprise of pop-up books. Choose those with texts that are rhythmic and repetitive. Show her the pictures but stay in charge of the page turning yourself to ensure the book survives the reading process. Most picture books for this age have few words so you can read them through quickly…perfect for an infant's short attention span.

> **Jan:** My granddaughter always enjoyed "reading" a small family photograph book that I assembled for her using an inexpensive plastic album. At ten months, she could point out Mommy, Daddy, Grandpa, Grammie and the family cat.

READING WITH TODDLERS

Young toddlers, like infants, may view a book as a toy—something to explore, flip through and manipulate. Older toddlers, on the other hand, linger longer with a book and may want to talk about the details of the illustrations. They savor the sounds, words and phrases heard again and again, and will often repeat some themselves. They might even want to hold the book independently and "read" to you or to their stuffed animals.

Toddlers have longer attention spans than infants, but it is still best to follow the child's lead as to how fast or thoroughly a book is read. Find a comfy chair or a sunny spot by the window where you can cuddle together and read. Some children want to read a book from cover to cover several times in one sitting; whereas others prefer to amble through the stories and pictures, conversing with you as they go. Even short books can take a long time when you are relaxed and cozy. Sometimes a child may talk about the tiniest details on the page and other times want to skip ahead to his favorite picture. Our advice? Flexibility with toddlers is always the key.

This is a good age to introduce your grandchild to the children's room of your local library. There may be story hours, author visits and reading clubs where children can collect prizes for completing reading lists. Children's librarians arrange story hours by age, so check the schedule.

While at the library, your grandchild is likely to pull out more books than he can carry on his own. Spread them out to review together. Book selection is an important part of the fun for a two-year-old so let him make his own choices of those to take home.

An older toddler may want to act out a story he has heard at story time. He may want to "trip, trap" down the walk like the Billy Goats Gruff or peek into that hole in your tree to see if there is honey for Winnie the Pooh. As you read, dramatize the story, exaggerate the sounds and emphasize the action. Remember, enthusiasm for books is infectious!

Lynne: In my most dramatic way, I read my children's dog-eared copy of *The Little Engine That Could* to my two-year-old grandson. I chugged and huffed up the hill like the little blue engine, slowly at first and then gaining speed. "I think I can, I think I can," was the refrain. Two weeks later my grandson grabbed my hand as we climbed up a hill. "Chug, Chug! I think I can, I think I can," he chanted...proving that the old classics never lose their charm.

To get you started, here are books that have been winners with our favorite toddlers.

• **Jez Alborough, *Where's My Teddy?*** A tale about a teddy bear mix-up.

• **Giles Andreae, *Giraffes Can't Dance*** A colorful book in which the giraffe hero finally succeeds.

• **Margaret Wise Brown, *The Runaway Bunny*** No matter what, Mommy would not let Baby get away.

• **Eric Carle, *The Very Hungry Caterpillar*** A beautiful surprise ending to a story of munching and counting.

- **Donald Crews, *Freight Train*** Simple story with few words and bold silhouettes about a train that comes, and then goes.

- **Peggy Rathmann, *Goodnight, Gorilla*** A funny story about a zoo-keeper and a mischievous gorilla.

- **Karma Wilson, *The Bear Snores On*** Repetition of the title phrase continues as the action unfolds in this story.

- **Audrey Wood, *The Napping House*** A picture book that features a snoring grandmother and a pesky flea.

- **Ellen Walsh, *Mouse Paint*** A delightful story of the antics of three mice with three jars of paint—red, yellow and blue. Good for learning how colors mix.

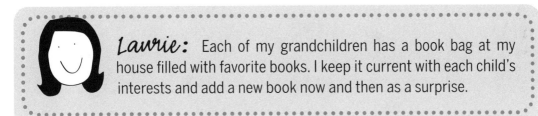

Laurie: Each of my grandchildren has a book bag at my house filled with favorite books. I keep it current with each child's interests and add a new book now and then as a surprise.

READING WITH PRESCHOOLERS

Studies have shown that children who are regularly exposed to books before they are two generally continue to enjoy them. However, books face fierce competition for children's attention from all types of electronic screens today. For children age three and beyond, maintaining an interest in reading is more of a challenge. You may be the key to making and keeping books an important part of your grandchild's future. The rewards are great. There is no substitute for the tactile pleasure of holding a real book and leafing through its pages at will; nor can the images on a screen replace the beautiful illustrations of a quality picture book.

Timing is important in engaging preschoolers with books. Notice what piques your grandchild's curiosity. The questions she asks about the world around her give you an opportunity to zero in on her interests and read books she is eager to hear. For example, after visiting a natural history museum with its amazing dinosaur exhibits, read her a book like Bernard Most's *ABC T-Rex*. Or a trip to the zoo can be followed by borrowing a library book about a favorite animal. If she is sick, bring her *Llama, Llama, at Home With Mama* by Anna Dewdney.

In general, what books should you have on hand for a preschooler? Seventy-five percent of a four-year-old's time is spent in fantasy play…she loves silly stories, fanciful rhymes and books about the preposterous and ridiculous which she can then use as a basis for her own imaginary play. The library is a good source of such funny and fantastic picture books.

Be prepared for her to request her favorites, again and again. After five or six times, she may be ready to "read" one back to you.

Lynne: Preschoolers can become obsessive about a topic or book. My grandson's unwavering love of Dr. Seuss's rhymes seemed to me to last forever but what a whiz he became at rhyming words!

Preschoolers are also fascinated by the "real" questions of life and want to learn facts relating to an amazing range of topics…how the human body works, what is in outer space and even about dying. You will find a host of age-appropriate books to cover these topics and answer her questions.

Beyond the fantasy and fact-filled, it is difficult to predict just which books a child will love. Offer lots of choices. Here is a list of books our preschool grandchildren have most enjoyed.

• **Keith Baker, *Who Is the Beast?*** This poor tiger learns, to his dismay, that he is the one others fear.

• **David Carter, *How Many Bugs in a Box?*** A pop-up counting book of strange bugs in boxes full of surprises.

• **Ed Emberley, *Go Away, Big Green Monster!*** A good book to read when the topic of monsters arises.

• **Katherine Holabird, *Angelina Ballerina*** The first of a series about a tutu-clad mouse who just cannot stop dancing.

- **Ezra Jack Keats, *The Snowy Day*** A story for snow day fun with a question at the end.

- **Laura Numeroff, *If You Give a Mouse a Cookie*** What preposterous things can happen if you give a mouse a cookie?

- **Beatrix Potter, *The Tale of Peter Rabbit*** Children love the escapades of curious, naughty Peter as he ventures into Mr. McGregor's garden.

- **Peggy Rathmann, *The Day the Babies Crawled Away*** A charming, rhyming story of infants who slip away from a picnic but are safely returned.

- **Dr. Seuss, *Horton Hatches the Egg*** A story telling what happens when a gentle elephant takes over for a lazy bird.

- **Maurice Sendak, *Where the Wild Things Are*** Who does not become a wild thing now and then?

- **Esphyr Slobodkina, *Caps for Sale*** A timeless tale about a peddler and a band of clever, mischievous monkeys.

- **Jane Yolen, *How Do Dinosaurs Say Goodnight?*** A fanciful picture book in which dinosaurs practice good bedtime behavior.

BRINGING STORIES TO LIFE

There are many ways to enhance story time. Sometimes your preschooler will just want to relax and listen as you read. At other times he will want to talk about the why's of something you read to him. Unlike his busy parents, you may have more time to deal with these seemingly endless questions about a story. Turn the question back to him now and then, and ask, "Why do YOU think that happened?"

Take your time reaching the end of the book. Pause to pay attention to the illustrations...are there clues your grandchild can use to predict what will happen next? By repeating refrains or guessing what is coming, he is building skills for reading comprehension.

- ACT OUT THE STORY with stuffed animals or puppets. You have probably already experimented with various voice tones and ranges of volume to make stories come alive. An older preschooler may want to draw a picture of his favorite character from a book or put on a little skit with you and Grandpa as the audience. For those children who are reluctant to take the stage, a puppet in hand may give him confidence to speak a few lines.

> *Jan:* When acting out *Goldilocks and the Three Bears* with my granddaughter, she wanted to change the ending. So Goldilocks stayed and played with Baby Bear, Mama Bear made more porridge, and Papa Bear fixed the broken chair. What creativity!

• SING-ALONG SONG BOOKS bring to life in pictures the tunes your grandchild knows by heart. Classic childhood songs like the *Wheels on the Bus* are in book form, making the tunes that have been loved by generations come alive visually. These books serve as good reminders of the lyrics and are an entertaining way for you and your grandchild to sing your way through the old favorites, perhaps even ones from your own childhood. Some have CDs included so your grandchild can listen as he reads or sings along. Our grandchildren have enjoyed these:

• **Pam Adams, *Old MacDonald Had a Farm***

• **Will Hillenbrand, *Down by the Station***

• **Bob Barner, *Dem Bones***

• **Sylvia Long, *Hush Little Baby***

• **Tom Birdseye, *She'll Be Coming 'Round the Mountain***

• REMEMBER TELLING STORIES AT BEDTIME in the dark with no book in your hand? If your storytelling skills are rusty, begin with familiar stories like *Three Billy Goats Gruff, Three Little Pigs* or *Goldilocks and the Three Bears*. No props are needed; just start with "Once upon a time..." and you are on your way.

• **START A STORY ABOUT YOUR GRANDCHILD** and see where it leads. Egocentric as they are, children of three and four love to hear stories about themselves. Begin, perhaps, like this: "There was a young boy/girl named (your grandchild's name) who had an exciting adventure. It started right in his/her own back yard. Just as (name) was watching a bluebird hopping from tree to tree, what do you suppose happened?" Let your grandchild help decide where the story goes from there as you both contribute ideas.

• **WHY NOT LET HIM WRITE HIS OWN BOOK?** Children love to see their ideas and experiences become stories in print. Seize opportunities such as the birth of a baby sister, the acquisition of a new puppy, or what you saw on an outing: "Shall we write a story about that? You say the words and I will write them down so we can remember just what happened. Would you like to draw a picture about that story? Shall we give it a title? Could we go read it to Grandpa or maybe post it on the refrigerator?" Date these keepsakes; you will be glad you captured these events in his own words. Seeing himself as an author helps your grandchild link the stories he has in his mind to those he loves in books.

• **YOUR GRANDCHILD MIGHT ALSO LIKE TO HEAR STORIES ABOUT HIS MOM OR DAD** when they were young. What were their favorite toys? Where did they like to go on vacation? And perhaps most intriguing, what mischievous things did they do? Imagine your son or daughter's surprise when hearing the tale retold by their own child!

Other rich sources to prompt storytelling could be a family heirloom, a treasured item from a trip or an old photograph. Here is your chance to share favorite tales and memories that are part of your family lore.

There is magic in reading a book or telling a story. Together you and your grandchild can travel as if on a magic carpet to another time and another world. Whether you are sitting together in the park or getting ready for bed, where will story time lead...to an imaginary land of fairies, to an adventure with dinosaurs, to the moon? Wherever it takes you, moments spent reading and sharing a book can be cherished times for you and your grandchild.

CHAPTER 7

YOUR GRANDCHILD, THE ARTIST

ART CAN BE MANY THINGS TO A CHILD—an outlet for creativity, a means of expressing ideas and emotions, a chance to experiment with new materials, an avenue for learning new words…truly an important part of a child's development. Best of all, art activities are fun.

An infant wants to touch, stroke, poke and squish everything to learn about her environment and uses art materials to that end. When she becomes a toddler, a child's artistic growth is reflected in her experiments with different media such as crayons, paint, clay and glue. She often goes overboard using too much glue, too much paint, too much of everything. By the time she is a preschooler, she has a better idea of how to use materials, has more control of her fine motor movements and her art may begin to take recognizable shape. In this chapter of art activities, there are no specific age suggestions; your grandchild's interest and skill level will determine how she approaches and completes them.

An adult's role should be providing space, time and materials and then allowing freedom of expression. What about coloring books? They can be convenient to have on hand but may restrict a child's imagination and creativity.

TIP: Dabbling in the arts can be messy. If you are worried about spills and spatters, set your grandchild up to work in a high chair, at a kitchen counter, at a covered table or seated on a plastic cloth on the floor. He will appreciate your company if you sit with him, but let the work be his own.

WHAT DOES YOUR ARTIST NEED?

Crayons, pencils and paints have been around forever and there is a reason…they continue to be the fundamental tools of children's art. However, today you will find a dizzying array of art supplies with special features for children. Some crayons and markers are washable; some are scented and appear glittery; some markers work only on companion paper; and glue now comes in sticks and dots.

OOPS! When you shop for artists under age five, choosing permanent markers could be a big mistake; select those with the washable label.

You do not need to have a completely stocked art studio to enjoy doing creative projects with your grandchild. Start simply and add materials as needed. Have lots of paper ready since very young artists work swiftly and, in spite of all the empty space you see on the page, that single zigzag may be his finished drawing.

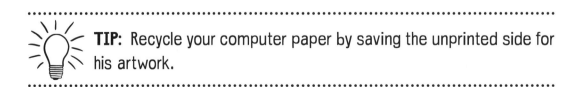

TIP: Recycle your computer paper by saving the unprinted side for his artwork.

In our experience, brand-name art products are generally better quality than cheaper substitutes and worth the extra expense. A stroll through your local craft store will offer you lots of choices. Here is a list to help you get started:

Basic Supply List

• CRAYONS – both fat and regular sizes

• PAPER – varying sizes and textures: computer paper, construction paper, old cards, junk mail, grocery bags, Post-It notes, cardboard, tagboard

• TEMPERA PAINT

• WATERCOLOR PAINT

• PAINT BRUSHES of assorted sizes (tempera paint needs sturdy brushes)

• MARKERS

• GLUE – liquid, glue sticks, paste

• OBJECTS TO GLUE – paper scraps, buttons, corks

• SIDEWALK CHALK

• PLAY DOUGH – two basic recipes in Appendix

• CHILD-SAFE SCISSORS – the ones with blunt ends that are designed to fit small hands

Nice-to-haves

• CLAY

• EASEL

• GLITTER/SEQUINS

• PAPER PLATES

- PAPER PUNCHES OF VARIOUS SHAPES

- RECYCLABLES – egg cartons, fabric scraps, Styrofoam, yarn, Popsicle sticks

- SOAP CRAYONS

- STICKERS

- STAMPS AND STAMP PADS

- WATERPROOF TABLE COVER

 TIP: Keep your art materials in a covered plastic tub or box so that they can be pulled out or put away easily.

Grammie's encouragement

Bite your tongue if you start to ask, "What is it?" Today's child development specialists tell us that to encourage artistic expression, it is far better to describe what you see. For example say, "You are using a lot of red," or "I see that your crayon goes up and down," or "It looks like you are working hard. You filled the whole page." This way of talking about a child's artwork may seem awkward at first, but experts remind us that children thrive on encouragement with specific observations, not general praise. It teaches them to value their own work rather than to rely on the reactions of others.

Do not expect your budding artist to dip a brush into paint and dab it on the paper as you would. He will do it his own way. For young children, the finished product is often unimportant. It is the process—the doing—that matters most to them.

Start by scanning the following categories for what appeals to you and what fits with the supplies you have on hand. Set up the project and let your grandchild begin. You will soon know what interests your artist and what is manageable for you. You will be on your way to building his very own art studio at Grammie's.

Laurie: I kept a folder of my grandchildren's creations, each one dated on the back. It made a wonderful collection and a record of their artwork over the years. When they wanted to take their work home, I snapped a picture for the file.

DRAWING

• CRAYON ART

Fat crayons are best for the younger child to grasp. At first she will move the crayon up and down, around and around and dot, dot, dot. An older child will eventually draw shapes—circles, crosses, squares. In time, these shapes will be recognizable as suns, houses, people.

Provide paper with different textures—rough sandpaper, slick freezer paper, bumpy or corrugated cardboard.

Turn a drawing into a masterpiece by backing it on a larger piece of colored paper or using a mat to frame it. To make a placemat, cover it with clear contact paper.

Bathtub art is the perfect activity for easy cleanup. All you need are soap crayons for body decorating and tub drawings and a willing artist in the water! Supervision required.

• RUBBINGS

Tape or lay a few flat objects such as a feather, key, coin, leaf or pine needle on a tray or counter top. Place a piece of paper over the objects and have your grandchild rub the paper with the SIDE of the crayon. The outline of the object will appear.

As a game, cover a secret object with paper and then ask your grandchild to rub with the crayon until she can guess what you hid.

• DECORATE A DRAWING

Invite your grandchild to embellish her drawing with stickers or stamps. Could this work of art be made into a greeting card or a bookmark?

Lynne: I've learned to always keep a small note pad and a pencil or two in my purse when I'm with my grandchildren. A quick game of tic-tac-toe or a chance to draw kept them busy if we had to wait to be served at a restaurant or arrived early for an appointment.

• TRACING

Set out cookie cutters and show your grandchild how to trace around one. She might like to try tracing around a little car, a block or shapes cut from stiff paper. Suggest she trace around your hand and then you trace hers.

• BODY TRACING

Place a large sheet of paper on the floor and have your grandchild lie on it on her back.

Trace around her body shape using a dark color crayon. By extending her arms up or bending her legs she will appear to be waving, jumping or running. After she has admired her image, encourage her to use crayons and markers to decorate the paper body and fill in facial features. Be sure to date the tracing.

Jan: I made life-sized dolls of each of my grandchildren when they turned three by transferring their body tracing from paper onto a double layer of fabric. Then I sewed around the edge, stuffed them, added yarn hair, drew a face and dressed the dolls in the children's outgrown clothes. The grandchildren wanted me to keep their "body-buddies" at my house so I wouldn't be lonesome. When they visited, it was fun to see how much the real children had grown.

• CHALK

Bring out the sidewalk chalk to decorate the driveway, play hopscotch or make roadmaps for toy cars. It is easy to hose off later. In fact, your grandchild might insist on doing the cleanup...rare is the young child who passes up a chance to squirt a hose!

Night Pictures (colored chalk on black paper) or Snow Scenes (white chalk on dark paper) are fun to make and also stimulate creative storytelling by young artists.

PAINTING

 TIP: One of Grandpa's old T-shirts or an old blouse of yours can make the perfect paint smock for your grandchild.

• TEMPERA

Tempera paint is the paint of choice for young children. It is water soluble, comes premixed, has a thick consistency and is available in a range of vivid colors. It will cover almost any surface that a child wants to paint—paper, wood, rocks or cardboard. Larger brushes work best.

Rock Art: Go looking for a few smooth stones, rub off any dirt and then paint them. Finish with a shake of glitter—a paperweight for Mom is a great gift!

Children love to paint just about anything...boxes of any size, corrugated cardboard, egg cartons, even foil.

• WATERCOLOR

Those familiar little paint sets are inexpensive and easy to use. Watercolor paints have a softer look than tempera and are best used on absorbent paper...try a paper towel. Smooth wood scraps also absorb the color for a durable piece of art.

Printing and blot painting with tempura

• FOLD A SHEET OF PAPER IN HALF AND CREASE IT Put a dollop of paint on the inside and re-fold. Pat or smooth the outside, then open it up for a surprise—sort of an inkblot effect. Try with heart-shaped or circle-shaped paper, too.

• TURN A MUFFIN TIN UPSIDE DOWN Paint the underside of the muffin tin and press it on paper for a polka dot print. Wash the tin and do again and again.

• CUT VEGGIES OR FRUITS IN HALF, dip them in a thin layer of paint and press firmly on paper to make a print. Interesting patterns can be made with bell peppers, potatoes, carrots, apples, oranges or even onions.

Painting without a paintbrush

• POUR TEMPERA PAINT into a shallow tray. Dip an object into the paint and print it on paper. Try a spatula, masher, fork, sponge, feather, tooth-pick, nylon puff or pipe cleaner. Can Grandpa guess what was used to make the design?

• PLACE A PIECE OF PAPER IN A SHALLOW BOX (large trays work, too) Drop a few marbles or golf balls into tempera paint then plop them onto the paper. Tip the box slowly to roll them around so that each leaves a paint trail. Repeat as needed for more color.

• DRIVE LITTLE CARS THROUGH A SHALLOW TRAY OF PAINT and then onto paper to make a colorful highway. Observe the tire patterns. Later give those cars a soapy "carwash" scrub.

• DIP A COTTON SWAB INTO A FOOD COLORING and water mixture and touch the tip onto a coffee filter or paper towel. Watch the color spread as it is being absorbed. Repeat with other colors. Hang the masterpiece in a window as a sun catcher, or glue it onto a larger piece of colored paper.

• HALF-FILL FOUR SECTIONS OF A MUFFIN TIN with water and help your grandchild add a few drops of food coloring to each—one yellow cup, one blue, one red, one green. Fold a paper towel or a half sheet of white tissue paper into a small square and have the child dip each corner into a different color. Call them "quick dips" to convey that the paper should not stay in the color very long. Lay the wet folded square on newspaper to dry and then unfold it for a colorful surprise. This homemade giftwrap makes the wrapping paper as special as the gift itself.

....

OOPS! Food coloring stains clothing, skin and countertops so cover your work surface and wear smocks or cover-ups.

....

• FINGER PAINTING

This is a wonderfully tactile but often messy experience. Buy finger paints or mix tempera paint with liquid starch (one part paint to two parts starch) to make your own. Spoon a dollop or two directly on a tray or paper that has been taped to the table so the paper will not move around as your grandchild begins to smear. Special paper can be purchased at craft stores, but the shiny side of freezer paper works just as well.

....

 TIP: If your grandchild is tentative at first to get his fingers in the paint, ask him if he can make a road through the paint with just one finger. He may then be willing to paint more wholeheartedly.

....

For another type of finger painting, try the edible version. Put a scoop of prepared instant pudding on a tray or plate and let your grandchild draw and lick. This approach might get a reluctant finger painter to try the idea...yummy!

• SHAVING CREAM PAINTING

Squirt some shaving cream onto a tray and watch him go—smearing, smearing—a different kind of finger painting. Bonus: "This smells like Daddy!"

• FACE PAINTING

When dipped in water, special crayons for face painting will decorate skin and wash off easily. Keep an unbreakable hand mirror nearby so your grandchild can watch as you paint his face with kitty whiskers or a red nose. Soon he will want to do it by himself.

OOPS! Allowing them to paint their own faces should only be done with older toddlers and preschoolers. Monitor the fun closely so that color stays out of the eyes and mouth. Have a damp cloth ready for quick cleanup. And beware: if you paint his face, he may want to paint yours!

GLUING, MAKING COLLAGES, AND CUTTING

As handy and tidy as glue sticks are, children need experience working with real glue. Since squeezing a bottle is difficult for young children, pour some glue into a shallow dish, and offer a cotton swab or small brush to use as an applicator.

 TIP: Out of glue? No problem. Simply make paste by mixing flour and water. Start with a 2:1 proportion of flour to water and thin to desired consistency.

• **COLLAGES** Make collages of paper scraps, uncooked pasta, beads, buttons, Cheerios, seashells, magazine pictures, cotton balls, ribbon, fabric scraps or maybe the treasures you gathered on a recent walk together. Use stiff bases such as cardboard, tag board, paper plates or foam meat trays from the grocery store.

• SCRAPBOOKING Thumb through magazines with your grandchild and cut or tear out pictures of cars, animals or whatever strikes her fancy. She can then glue them into a "book" of plain sheets of paper you have stapled together.

• GLITTER ART Children love glitter. Here is a secret for easy clean up. Help your grandchild brush small items like rocks, leaves or pine cones with glue and, one at a time, put them in a brown paper bag with glitter already in it. Close the bag and have your grandchild give it a few shakes— good glitter coverage and minimal mess!

• GOT PASTA? Place uncooked pasta of interesting shapes in a clear plastic bag. Add drops of food coloring, secure the bag and ask your grandchild to shake it until the pasta is colored to her satisfaction. Spread on toweling to dry. On another day, use it for gluing collages or stringing as necklaces or bracelets.

• SPAGHETTI PLOPS After a spaghetti dinner, turn cooked leftover pasta into an art project. Color the pasta in a plastic bag with food coloring. Shake and shift pasta around until desired color is reached (several squirts of food coloring may be needed). Drop or plop strand by strand onto a paper plate or stiff paper base for a free form design or twist strands into shapes or letters. The pasta sticks to the paper and dries with a hard plastic appearance.

• EGGSHELL MOSAICS Save your eggshells from colored Easter eggs. Dry them, crush them a bit, and let your grandchild glue the shell pieces onto colored paper. You might add other collage materials to complete the art piece such as Styrofoam pellets or Easter grass.

• PAPER PUNCHES Today paper punches are available that work by pushing down rather than by squeezing. These are generally easier for children to use and are designed to produce a variety of shapes. Save the cutouts to use later for a confetti toss or to add to a collage.

• CUTTING IS A CHALLENGING SKILL THAT TAKES PRACTICE Start simply with a pair of children's scissors and a narrow strip of paper. Hold the strip taut while your grandchild cuts with quick snips. Next, draw broad straight or curvy lines on construction paper as a cutting "map" for your grandchild to follow. Eventually she will be ready to cut pictures out of old magazines or cut around a shape or picture she drew herself.

SCULPTING AND BUILDING

• PLAY DOUGH

Play dough is widely available for purchase or can be easily made at home. It will keep for weeks if stored airtight. If homemade, add a couple drops of vanilla or peppermint extract for a scented experience or glitter for some sparkle. See recipes in Appendix.

Most children squish, poke, pound and roll play dough at first. Do not expect your grandchild to make something recognizable; it is the tactile experience that he enjoys.

A little rolling pin, Popsicle sticks, plastic dishes, garlic press, cookie cutters or plastic figures are props that add a new dimension to the play.

Snipping play dough is another good way to use those child-safe scissors.

• GOOP

An easy, messy, oozy freeform mixture of corn starch and water. See Appendix for instructions.

• CLAY SCULPTURE AND MODELING

Clay offers a different tactile experience. Purchase it at art or craft stores. It keeps indefinitely in a sealed plastic bag. If it dries out, poke little wells in the clay, add a few drops of water and reseal in a plastic bag for several hours before using.

Since it is a bit messy, cover the work surface with oilcloth or heavy plastic cloth. As your grandchild works, keep a dish of water handy to rinse hands or to moisten or smooth the clay.

Clay objects will air dry and can then be painted. To further preserve them as keepsakes, paint on a top coat of a one-to-one mixture of white glue and water.

TIP: For the latest in modeling products, visit your local craft store or research on Google.

• TOOTHPICK SCULPTURE

Connect toothpicks with slightly thawed frozen peas. As the peas dry they will harden and hold the toothpicks in place.

Try this same building technique using miniature marshmallows.

• BUILDING WITH SMALL BOXES

 Save small boxes such as the ones from checkbooks, jewelry, toothpaste or greeting cards. Provide glue and tape to make tiny garages, animal homes, towers or whatever your grandchild imagines. Decorate with paint, markers or stickers.

• BUILDING WITH LARGE BOXES

Did you purchase a new refrigerator or water heater lately? The packing box can become a fort, store, house or cave. Your grandchild may need your help to decorate with paints and markers. Make the inside cozy using blankets or towels for rugs and tape his artwork on the walls.

RECYCLING AS ART

• STYROFOAM

Though we know it is environmentally unfriendly, if you have it, use it and reuse it. Here are some ways:

Peanuts and smaller pieces can be used for gluing in collages. Some of the packing pellets are biodegradable and become sticky "worms" when quickly dipped in water. They will then stick to each other to make interesting shapes. If left in water they will eventually disintegrate…magic!

If large chunks of Styrofoam are available, your grandchild can paint them and then add toothpicks, pipe cleaners or small twigs to make a boat or spaceship or houses for little animals.

• PAPER TUBES

Binoculars: Tape two toilet paper tubes together side-by-side. Decorate with drawings or stickers. Attach a piece of yarn so the binoculars can be worn around the neck. They really do help a child focus on an object.

Telescope: Decorate a paper towel tube and practice looking through it with one eye. Do not be surprised when your grandchild finds other uses for it, such as a sword or a horn…she is just using her imagination.

Rain sticks: Tape one end of a paper towel tube tightly closed. Have your grandchild fill it half full with tiny pebbles, rice, dried corn or beans. Securely tape the other end closed. Decorate it, and ta-da… a shaker for a band or a rain dance!

Jan: One day the twins and I dipped the ends of paper tubes in glue and set them upright on a cardboard base. I cut out colorful paper circles for roofs and suddenly we had little houses. One twin made pebble paths and snowy bushes out of cotton balls; the other added cork people. It sparked their imaginations about who might live in this village. "This is my house. You can be my neighbor."

• EGG CARTONS

Painting: It is fun to paint the uneven surface of an egg carton. Once dry, it can become a treasure chest.

For collecting: Take one along on a walk to collect tiny rocks, small leaves or flower petals. Close the lid so those treasures make it all the way home.

For sorting games, use beads, dried beans, cotton puffs or pebbles. How many different ways can the objects be sorted into the egg carton's little cups—by color, by shape, by size?

Caterpillars: Cut the bottom of an egg carton in half lengthwise making two long strips. Decorate the bumps. Add toothpicks or pipe cleaner antennas and googly eyes for a one-of-a-kind caterpillar.

Bells: Cut an egg carton into individual cups and decorate each one. Poke a pipe cleaner or ribbon through the cup, attach a little bell and it becomes an instrument or an ornament.

• CORKS

Corks can be used for collage projects or stacked to make high towers.

Dip in tempera paint and then stamp on paper to make a pattern.

• PAPER GROCERY BAGS

Cut them so they open flat for painting, gluing and drawing.

Make a fabulous hat. Turn a brown paper grocery bag inside out and, working slowly, roll up the edges leaving a crown for the top of the head. The paper hat can be scrunched into many stylish shapes which can be decorated with feathers, flowers, stickers and markers. This creates a sort of Mad Hatter look which might inspire a crazy hat contest.

• STALE BREAD

To make a bird feeder, your grandchild can cut stale sandwich bread into shapes using large cookie cutters. Dry out the bread in a low temperature oven. Push a plastic straw through the bread to cut a little hole for attaching a string or pipe cleaner hanger. Then spread peanut butter or vegetable shortening on one side. Place sticky side down into a shallow pan of birdseed to coat it and hang it where she can watch the birds feast.

SEASONAL CELEBRATIONS AND HOLIDAYS

These activities are grouped into seasons but are fun to do any time of year.

Spring

• CENTERPIECES Gather sticks, pine cones, seashells, flowers, pebbles, feathers, pipe cleaners and/or toothpicks. Push into a block of oasis (the porous, foam-like material used in flower arranging).

• FLOWER PRINTING Dip a single flower blossom into shallow paint and then dab it repeatedly on paper.

• **COLORING EGGS** With hard boiled eggs, food coloring, water and a little vinegar, you can color eggs any time of year—use flag colors for the Fourth of July, pink or red for Valentine's Day, or orange for jack-o'-lantern faces in the fall.

• **CROWNS** Size a strip of paper to fit around your grandchild's head. Let him decorate it according to the season or whim of the day with hearts, stars, leaves, stickers or sparkles. Staple or tape closed and crown your royal majesty.

• **HATS** Cut a large circle (about twenty inches in diameter) from sturdy paper such as brown wrapping or shelf paper. Have your grandchild decorate it using markers, crayons or stickers. Center the paper on his head. Hold it in place as you wrap it with masking tape so that it fits his head in the shape of the crown of a hat. You will need to take tucks in the paper as you wrap. Roll or scrunch the brim to create the look he wants—is he a firefighters, a pirate, a forest ranger, or...?

• **BASKETS** Weave ribbon, yarn or colored strips of paper in and out of the holes of a plastic berry basket to make a container for spring flowers, colored eggs or shiny pebbles. A pipe cleaner handle is the final touch.

Summer

• **ICE PLAY** Purchase a large block of ice and place it on a tray to catch drips. A sprinkle of rock salt (available at the grocery store) will create craters in the ice which become even more interesting with a few drops of food coloring. Add more salt, more color, more salt, more color and watch what happens.

Make your own ice shapes by freezing water in milk cartons, bowls or cake pans. Before freezing, add food coloring, flowers, leaves or a small plastic toy. When frozen, unmold and use rock salt to make the craters. Other ice cubes or chunks will stick to the larger one to build ice castles, igloos or towers.

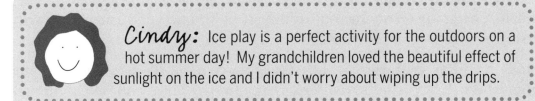
• WRAPPING Let your grandchild wrap up anything he treasures such as a special rock, pine cone or toy. Use recycled wrapping paper, one of his own drawings or newspaper for the giftwrap. You may need to help by cutting the paper to a manageable size or tearing off pieces of tape.

TIP: Using tape can be frustrating for young children. As an alternative, use foil as the wrapping paper. It will stay put when wrapped around an object.

• PAPER CHAINS Cut colored paper into strips about one-and-one-half inches by six inches. Tape the first strip into a loop, then link on the next strip and continue on. Very young children may only be able to thread the next strip into the circle but older children will soon master the technique. Tape is easier to manage than staplers. Use as a decoration over the doorway, on the table or hung from a tree.

• FLAGS Decorate flag-sized pieces of muslin or old white sheeting with felt markers or diluted food coloring. Attach with masking tape to a stick or dowel and you have a grand old flag for marching about.

Fall

• LEAVES Collect leaves to paint, glue and glitter.

• PUMPKINS If they are not carved, pumpkins can live on after Halloween. Paint them, wash off and paint again. Decorate one for a special centerpiece. The mini-pumpkins are especially good for this activity.

- **PINE CONES** Make a bird feeder by spreading peanut butter or vegetable shortening on a pine cone, rolling it in birdseed and hanging it with string or wire from a tree branch.

Make a turkey centerpiece. Lay the pine cone on its side and let your grandchild stick feathers, real or paper, into the large end. Then glue on a paper turkey head. These pine cone turkeys can be used to hold place cards, too.

Turn a pine cone into a tree. Set it upright on a stiff base or paper plate (a ball of play dough or clay will help hold it in place). Decorate with paints, yarn, beads and glitter.

Winter

- **STAMPING** Place cookie cutters in a shallow amount of tempera paint and then stamp them over and over onto paper.

Cut kitchen sponges into simple shapes such as triangles, squares and circles. Moisten shapes with water and squeeze well. Dip in shallow paint and use to stamp on paper. Holiday shapes are fun, too—hearts, trees and stars.

- **CUTTING** Bring out old greeting cards and catalogs for cutting. Your grandchild will go to town snipping out pictures of animals, people and the toys he loves.

Make snowflakes with circular coffee filters (the type that look like large cupcake liners) or from white paper cut into circles. Help your grandchild fold the circle in half (looks like a taco), then in half again (looks like a snow cone), and then fold once more (looks like an ice cream cone). Holding it folded, he can cut little scallops or triangle shapes along any of the edges or folds, including the bottom tip. Be careful he does not cut through the entire cone shape. Unfold and behold the lacy snowflake.

Fold a piece of construction paper in half. Draw half of the shape you desire on the paper with the midline on the fold. Shapes that work well are hearts, trees, egg shapes and pumpkins. Have your grandchild cut out the shape following the outline on the paper. Open the folded paper and the whole object appears, almost magically.

• TREE DISCS The ends that are trimmed off Christmas trees at tree lots make wonderful natural bases for art work. Most tree lots are happy to give them to you. Use as bases for pinecone art or glue on small objects from nature—pebbles, greens, seashells or twigs.

• ICE WREATH If you have cold winters, freeze water in an angel food or bundt pan with holly sprigs or cranberries. Unmold, take it outside and tie to a branch with ribbon for an icy wreath.

ARTFUL GIFTS

Children love to give gifts especially when an element of surprise is involved. You can easily turn many of the previously suggested art projects into special gifts...simply wrap and present. Here are a few other ideas:

• FLOWER POTS Paint a clay flowerpot with patio paint which is available at most crafts stores. Turn the pot upside down before starting to be sure that the outside is painted instead of the inside!

• HANDPRINTS make wonderful gifts in a variety of ways. A simple tracing of your grandchild's hand can be used on the front of a card or as a framed memory. Paint the palm of her hand (or the bottoms of her feet) with fabric paint for a lasting imprint on a dishtowel, apron or T-shirt. Remember the kindergarten clay handprint your children made all those years ago?

• FABRIC PENS can be used to decorate a pillowcase for Mom or Dad.

• **GREETING CARDS** Draw pictures or use stamp art or stickers on blank note cards to make stationery.

• **PICTURE FRAMES** Glue seashells, buttons, tiny pebbles or jewels on a simple wood frame.

• **FOR AN ART OUTING** with a little expense involved, visit a ceramics store to see what is available for young children to paint.

Have we sparked your inner artist? Hopefully you will find it fun to pick a project, improvise with materials you have on hand, and follow your grandchild's lead. Be sure to reserve room on your refrigerator or a spot on the mantel...little artists rarely stop at just one masterpiece.

CHAPTER 8

MILES APART...
YET **CLOSE AT HEART**

RELATIONSHIPS REQUIRE CARE AND NURTURING. SOME OF US ARE BLESSED TO BE PART OF OUR GRANDCHILD'S DAILY OR WEEKLY LIFE because we live close to one another. We get invited to dinner or just pop in now and then for a quick hello and our "Grammie fix." However, according to a recent American Association of Retired Persons (AARP) report, half of all grandparents in America live more than 200 miles from their grandchildren. If this is your situation, what can you do to share your love across the miles?

It takes conscious, sustained and special effort. Not only do you need to plan ahead for visits and phone calls but you will be making frequent trips to the post office. You may also want to learn about the latest in video chatting and update your skills to take advantage of new technology.

Planning ahead

Long-distance grandparenting does not lend itself to the luxury of last-minute action. If you do not shop for gifts well in advance of birthdays, for instance, your presents will arrive late. You could shop online near the special date but you will face steep expediting charges. If you rely on spur-of-the-moment phone calls, you could be disappointed to reach only voicemail.

Laurie: I needed reminders two or three weeks ahead to mail off something to my grandchildren who live far away. Those red circles on the calendar jogged my memory so gifts arrived on time.

Using what's new

The many recent advances in technology can be great assets in spanning the miles between homes. Nothing can take the place of hugging, tickling or kissing your grandchild. However, being able to see and talk with each other in real time on a screen has, for many grammies, a distinct advantage over traditional phone calls.

Connecting this way requires equipment such as a computer, smart phone or webcams. To keep up with the rapidly evolving field of electronic communication, talk with experts for their recommendations: your computer-savvy children, friends with experience in using these "new-fangled gadgets" or a salesperson in an electronics store.

TIP: Before you invest in new technology, be sure your children want to communicate this way and have compatible equipment so you can share waves and smiles and blow those kisses from here to there!

KEEPING IN TOUCH WITH INFANTS

• ASK YOUR SON OR DAUGHTER to help you stay present in your grandchild's life by talking about you and keeping your photograph in the baby's view. It is surprising that even a child under one year of age can recognize faces in pictures.

 TIP: Do you have a favorite name you want your grandchild to call you—Grammie, or Gigi, or Boppy, or Nana, or Oma, or Nonnie or Grandma Sue? This is the time to claim it and ask your children to use it as they talk about you.

• LAMINATE SMALL PHOTOGRAPHS of yourself so your grandchild can play with them and see your face often.

• EMAIL OR PHONE her parents frequently so they can update you on your grandchild's growth and new skills.

• SEND LITTLE PRESENTS Surprises are welcome any time of year; no need to wait for a birthday or special occasion. Newborns and infants like soft and colorful stuffed animals, simple rattles and toys with tactile appeal. Cloth books and small board books make good gifts, too.

• DIG OUT AND MAIL PHOTOGRAPHS of your own child when he or she was your grandchild's age. It is fun for everyone to see if there is a family resemblance.

KEEPING IN TOUCH WITH TODDLERS

As your grandchild reaches toddlerhood, he can probably now identify you in photographs and refers to you by that special name. He may remember you from one internet session or phone call to the next. Depending on how often he has seen you, he may or may not welcome you readily when you arrive for a visit.

By phone or screen

- SPONTANEOUS CALLS (if you find your grandchild at home) can be fun. These are the calls that are just made on the fly to say "hi" and tell him you are making cookies or that it snowed last night. These are very short conversations to share your daily lives.

- SCHEDULED CALLS, perhaps just after dinner or on Saturday morning, are convenient for many families. If you establish a regular time to call, be sure to stick with it so your grandchild can look forward to hearing from you.

OOPS! Time zones make a difference. Be sure you adjust for HIS time before you call.

- PHONE CONVERSATIONS WITH A TODDLER can be one-sided and unpredictable. Some older, more verbal toddlers will talk easily on the phone; others may "freeze" and say nothing or only "Hi." Even if all you hear is his breathing or tiny giggles, it will still make your day and he will be hearing your voice.

 TIP: You will have a better chance for a longer conversation if you avoid asking questions that can be answered with a simple yes or no. Instead of asking, "Did you go to the park today?", ask "What did you do at the park?" Be patient and wait a bit before asking another question; he may take a long time to answer.

- A TODDLER IS LEARNING THE SOUNDS different animals make. He will probably respond if you ask "What does the cow say? How does the kitty talk?" and be sure to let him show you how clever he is with his "moos" or "meows."

- SING A SONG your grandchild knows such as *Twinkle, Twinkle, Little Star* or *Old MacDonald Had a Farm*. If you get it started, he may join in.

By mail

Toddlers love to receive their own mail. Although email has become the mode of written communication for many of us, do not underestimate the impact of snail mail for children. A card in the mail is something tangible, just for them; it can be carried around and looked at again and again.

• MUSICAL GREETING CARDS that play a song when they are opened are a great hit with this age.

• SEND LITTLE PACKAGES OR LETTERS that include some stickers or colorful pictures from a magazine.

• IF YOU OWN A DOG OR CAT, have Fido or Fluffy write your grandchild a letter and include a picture.

• GLUE A SMALL PHOTOGRAPH of yourself and Grandpa on the inside of a card where the signature would normally be. Your grandchild can then open the card and "read" who sent the greetings.

• TAKE PICTURES AND MAKE A SMALL PHOTOGRAPH ALBUM...of you and your grandchild, of you and Grandpa, of times you have shared. Pop it in the mail to him and talk about it when you call.

Cindy: I made a personal story book for my granddaughter with pictures of the two of us taken during a recent visit. I wrote very simple sentences on each page. Her parents said that for weeks it was the only book she wanted to read. A few months later when I was visiting her house, she "read" the book to me. What fun that was for both of us!

• ASK YOUR SON OR DAUGHTER TO MAKE A TEMPLATE of your grandchild's high chair tray and send it to you. Trace it on colorful paper and make a photograph collage of him, you and Grandpa. Add some stickers, laminate it, and mail it back to entertain him at mealtime. When he graduates from high chair to table, make placemats the same way.

• RECORD YOURSELF READING A FAVORITE BOOK There are books for sale today (even in grocery stores) that make it possible to record your voice without special equipment. Some greeting cards have this capability, too.

KEEPING IN TOUCH WITH PRESCHOOLERS

Now a more willing communicator, the preschooler wants to stay in touch with her favorite people. She may want to punch in your number, send you a picture she has drawn or talk with you at great length about anything and everything. She is now building a memory bank of times you have shared and will remind you about them: "Remember when you spilled the Cheerios? Remember when I slept in your big bed? Remember when we had lunch at the airport?"

By phone

• ASK TO SPEAK SPECIFICALLY WITH YOUR GRANDCHILD when you phone her house. Can you imagine how important a child feels when the phone rings and it is for HER?

• TIMING IS IMPORTANT Call when she is most likely to want to talk on the phone. It might be hard for a preschooler to break away from a play date, even for a chat with you.

 TIP: Practice makes perfect when it comes to phone calls. As you call her more frequently and she gets used to phone conversations, your preschooler will likely become more chatty.

By mail

• PRINT IN BLOCK LETTERS when sending mail. Your grandchild is beginning to recognize the letters of the alphabet and will see her name in the address.

• PRESCHOOLERS LIKE TO WATCH FOR THE MAILMAN Send a note regularly with a surprise inside: a picture, a gift certificate for her local bookstore or washable tattoos. If you enclose a self-addressed, stamped envelope, you will be more likely to get a note in return.

Laurie: To stay in touch with my out-of-town grandson, I decided to send him a note every Sunday. When I used the regular mail, I selected from my stash of cute cards; then I only needed to add a quick message, the address, and a stamp. I also subscribed to an e-card service so when I used email for my weekly greeting, my message was colorful and animated.

• SEND BLANK, SELF-ADDRESSED, STAMPED POSTCARDS inside a bigger envelope. Ask your grandchild to decorate the postcards and mail them to you. When you receive one, have Grandpa take a picture of YOU getting it out of your mailbox or displaying it on your refrigerator. Send the photograph back to complete the connection.

• CARRY A FEW POSTCARD STAMPS in your purse so it is easy to buy and send a card to just say "hi" from any interesting place you visit.

• MAIL A GIFT TO ACCOMPANY A STORY she enjoys, such as a red hat for *Little Red Riding Hood,* mittens for *The Snowy Day* or a teddy bear for the tale of *Goldilocks and the Three Bears.* A little surprise arriving for no special reason is a wonderful way to let your grandchild know you are thinking of her.

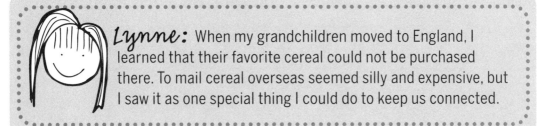

Lynne: When my grandchildren moved to England, I learned that their favorite cereal could not be purchased there. To mail cereal overseas seemed silly and expensive, but I saw it as one special thing I could do to keep us connected.

• **HOW ABOUT EMAILING PHOTOGRAPHS** from your digital camera that show what you and Grandpa have been doing?

• **MAIL HER A DISPOSABLE CAMERA** and ask her to be the photographer taking pictures for you of her room, family and toys.

When you're together

• **PLANT A SMALL BUSH OR TREE** the next time she visits. Take pictures of it in different seasons and send them to her. Then you can watch both the tree and your grandchild grow.

Jan: When we learned there was a rosebush named Queen Elizabeth, we planted it for our granddaughter Elizabeth. A few years later, of course we had to have the "Princess" Caroline, followed by the "Lady" Anne. When the three girls visit, you can be sure they carefully inspect their own namesake plant to see if it's blooming.

• **HELP YOUR GRANDCHILD DECORATE A SHOEBOX** for the letters and pictures you exchange. Use heart stickers or photographs of both of you to help her remember that this box contains love notes from you and Grandpa.

• **CREATE A FAMILY CALENDAR** with a different photograph memory for each month. Photography stores or web photograph services can help. Remember to include the dog and cat…they are part of the family, too.

Surprise of the month

Why not send something every month? Nothing lavish or expensive...just a reminder that you are thinking of her.

• In JANUARY, when it is cold and blustery, send hot cocoa mix and some marshmallows.

• When FEBRUARY comes, it is time for valentines.

• For windy days in MARCH, send a kite or have Grandpa make a paper airplane to mail.

• In APRIL, how about mailing an egg coloring kit and plastic eggs to hide?

• You could send seeds to plant in MAY.

• She would love a colorful beach towel to celebrate JUNE, the beginning of summer.

• In JULY, package up a small American flag, patriotic stickers and a CD of music for marching...send to arrive before the Fourth.

• Gift certificates to a favorite ice cream store would be perfect on a hot AUGUST day.

• Send a box of crayons and some paper in SEPTEMBER so she can capture the fall colors.

• In OCTOBER, Halloween napkins, paper plates and stickers would be welcome.

• A book about Thanksgiving will help her celebrate that NOVEMBER holiday.

• In DECEMBER, how about a pair of cozy, warm socks or mittens with a snowflake or snowman design?

MAKING VISITS SPECIAL

Of course, the most satisfying experience for you, Grammie, is actually being with your grandchild whether at his house or yours. Visit your grandchild as often as you are invited and are able and be sure his family knows they have an open invitation to your home, too.

Keep in mind:

• YOU AND YOUR FAMILY MAY CHOOSE TO PLAN VISITS AROUND SPECIAL GATHERINGS such as a birthday party, holiday or family celebration. Or it may be preferable to get together when it is less busy and there is more unscheduled time available.

• ANY OVERNIGHT GUEST CHANGES THE NORMAL ROUTINE of a household. When visiting them, your children may appreciate your offer to stay at a nearby motel, especially if space at their house is limited.

• YOUR GRANDCHILD MAY NEED TIME TO WARM UP TO YOU when he first sees you. Do not be surprised if he is a little shy. Let him make the first move and you will soon find that he is bringing you his favorite blankie and books to read.

Now for the fun...think about how you might include activities in your visits which create memories just between the two of you. Plan things he will always look forward to doing with you, when visiting in either direction.

When Grammie visits me, she always:

• HIDES SMALL GIFTS FOR ME IN HER SUITCASE

• TAKES ME FOR ICE CREAM

• PLAYS HIDE-AND-SEEK WITH ME

• LETS ME CRAWL INTO BED WITH HER IN THE MORNING

When I go to Grammie's house, we always:

- MAKE PLAY DOUGH

- TAKE WALKS

- RING THE DINNER BELL

- GO TO HER FAVORITE PARK

- BAKE A SPECIAL CAKE

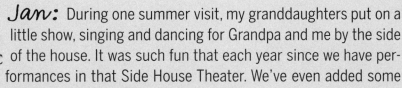

Jan: During one summer visit, my granddaughters put on a little show, singing and dancing for Grandpa and me by the side of the house. It was such fun that each year since we have performances in that Side House Theater. We've even added some lighting and seats and now we all take part!

It is not easy to be far away from a grandchild. Building bridges that span the miles may take effort and persistence, but it can be done. Pick up the phone and call regularly. Keep the mailman busy. Share moments on a screen (one of the few good applications of technology for children this age). Find what works for you and be consistent with your communication. Even if you and your grandchild live miles apart, you can stay close at heart.

CHAPTER 9

AND NOW FOR GRANDPA

GRANDPAS ARE GREAT! DOES THE MAN AT YOUR HOUSE KNOW THIS and how much his grandchild would love to play with him? Does he realize how much his grandfatherly attention could mean to that little one and the impact he could have on his grandchild's life? If some encouragement is needed to get him involved, invite or even nudge him to try some of the grandpa-tested activities in this chapter. He will thank you later.

Some things have changed

Many men are eager to welcome a grandchild. Others, quite frankly, do not feel ready to embrace this new role because, in sync with today's youth-obsessed culture, their mental image of a grandfather does not match their vision of themselves. The average American grandfather has his first grandchild before he is 50, far from the stereotype of the old man with the white mustache and a cane. At this age, most men are still working. Many maintain a healthier lifestyle than the grandfathers of yesteryear and are technology-savvy with smart phones and computers. Ah, but ready or not, when his own grandchild climbs up onto his lap and calls him Grandpa, that name feels pretty darn good.

Today's grandpas may not have had much involvement in the daily care of their own children because of jobs and career commitments. In fact, these grandfathers may have missed out on some of the highlights in their own children's lives. Grandchildren give them a second chance to share their skills and actively participate in the life of a young child…a kind of "do-over" parenting.

In many families today, children are used to having both parents meet their daily needs. With either dad or mom changing diapers, feeding and playing with their children, grandfathers as well as grandmothers have an open door to become totally involved. Young children are eager, curious and ready for grandfathers to spend time with them and teach the special skills men typically master, such as playing ball, fixing what is broken or building a snowman. Do not let your husband miss out. Now is the perfect time for him to share who he is and what he knows with this new generation.

GRANDFATHERING STYLES

Grandfathers come in many different shapes and sizes, and the ways they relate to their grandchildren are as varied as their personalities. However, here are four general styles to consider:

• THE FUN-LOVING GRANDFATHER is playful and informal. He enjoys playing like a child and encourages his grandchildren to be outgoing and physical. This grandpa may like to play Peek-A-Boo with an infant, swing on the swings with a toddler and have a snowball fight with a preschooler.

• THE HOW-TO GRANDFATHER is the one who introduces new skills and coaches progress. This grandpa enjoys teaching an infant how to roll a ball, a toddler how to pedal a bike and the preschooler how to plant a garden.

• THE HESITANT GRANDFATHER interacts with his grandchild in the same way an uncle or a family friend might. He may need an invitation and suggestions on how to get involved. By carrying his infant grandchild around the house and introducing her to the pictures on the walls, this grandfather will slowly gain confidence and feel more comfortable. He can work on a puzzle with a toddler and introduce a preschooler to the wonders of binoculars.

• THE READY-AND-WILLING GRANDFATHER knows how to completely care for a child for an afternoon or even a weekend. He can lull an infant to sleep, cook macaroni and cheese with a toddler or wash the car with a preschooler...all without a second thought.

The masculine approach

With little children, men are often sillier, more physical and less constrained than women...little ones like that. They love to hear Grandpa's deeper voice, explore his scratchy face, watch him shave or simply follow him around.

Cindy: I was my granddad's buddy from morning until night. He included me in many simple things he did each day... from fixing bacon at breakfast, to grocery shopping or bailing water from the boat after a rain. I still treasure those memories.

Grandfathers are often keepers of routines. They have a range of tasks each day: taking out the trash, walking the dog, bringing in the mail, watering the plants. Even a small child can help with these daily chores, gaining, as he does them, a sense of responsibility. More importantly, he is having fun with Grandpa.

Grandpas enjoy their toys as much as children like theirs. Sharing grown-up toys (cameras, model trains, remote control planes, fishing gear, sports equipment or carpentry tools) gives them an easy way to connect with their grandchildren. These interactions can be a springboard for many happy times.

Laurie: There's a room in our house called Grandpa Dick's Museum. He travels widely and brings home unusual souvenirs from all over the world...from Tibetan yak bells to New Guinea nose ornaments. The grandchildren love to hear his stories of where and how he found them.

Grandparents universally want their grandchildren to succeed in life. However, it is often the grandfathers who take on the role of teaching a healthy work ethic and the skills children need as adults. Men promote responsibility and like to help their grandchildren with practical matters like using simple carpentry tools safely, keeping the sidewalk clean and basic money management.

Cindy: Granddad emptied his pockets of spare change each night and saved the coins in a shoebox for his holiday visits with us. He dumped out the coins on a sheet and we grandchildren spent hours sorting and counting them. He never failed to remind us of the importance of saving for a rainy day.

For those grandfathers with an interest in photography, taking pictures is an easy way to get involved with young children. With today's digital cameras, there is no waiting for the results so children can view the photograph right away and enjoy their own silly faces. By taking picture after picture, Grandpa can be the family historian, at least for that day.

Laurie: To mark the passage of time in our family, Grandpa Dick measured each grandchild's growth over the years. Rather than marking up a door frame, he made a growth chart out of a six-foot long, one-inch by six-inch piece of lumber. He recorded the height of each grandchild including their name, age and date. Even if we move, that chart can go with us.

GRANDPA WITH INFANTS

Infants have traditionally been women's business because usually women feel more at ease with infants than men do. However as we cared for and played with our grandchildren, we tried to make sure our husbands were involved from the very first.

 *Jan:* Once Grandpa Dave learned how to support our newborn granddaughter's head, he realized she wasn't going to break and felt more comfortable holding and talking to her. And so began the first of many heart-to-heart conversations.

Here are some suggestions for the grandpa in your house on how to get up close and personal with new infants:

Inside the house, Grandpa can:

• TAKE A WALK-AND-TALK TOUR throughout the house telling the new baby about what he sees. This gives her a chance to get used to Grandpa's voice and touch.

• TALK AND WAVE AT THE BABY IN A MIRROR Infants are fascinated with the moving images.

• SING ANY SONG TO THE BABY It can be a lullaby or the Marines' Hymn—what Baby loves is the rhythm, the repetition and that deep voice.

• GIVE HER A BOTTLE OR BURP HER after a feeding. Many grandfathers like to feel they are doing something constructive.

• PLAY PEEK-A-BOO OR PAT-A-CAKE The more Baby and Grandpa interact the more comfortable they will be with each other.

• SOOTHE HIS FUSSY GRANDCHILD BY BOUNCING HER gently or cuddling with her in a rocking chair. Grandpa may earn the title of Baby Whisperer.

• HOLD HER AND DANCE AROUND THE FLOOR to a waltz or tango…even if Grandpa has two left feet.

• STACK SOFT BLOCKS as high as possible. Can he get to five before the baby knocks them down?

• READ ALOUD while holding her on his lap. Does Grandpa know that the experts say this will encourage future literacy even for an infant?

Jan: Seeing Grandpa Dave read to our infant grandchildren always made me smile. Rather than scurrying around to find a children's book, he would simply hold the baby and continue reading what interested him. It might have been just the morning paper. Of course that didn't matter; the baby was content sitting on his lap and hearing his voice.

• CHANGE A DIAPER Give Grandpa a demonstration so there is no excuse. He really can do it!

Going outside, Grandpa can:

• WALK AROUND WITH BABY in his arms and describe the cars going by, trees, plants, birds and clouds…fun for both and a welcome respite for a busy grammie or the new parents.

• TAKE BABY FOR A WALK in the carriage or stroller…a great way to soothe a fussy infant.

• BLOW SOAP BUBBLES and watch with Baby as they float away.

• RUN AN ERRAND in the car and take Baby along…but be sure to check first with her parents and follow all the safety rules for traveling with an infant in the car.

GRANDPA WITH TODDLERS

Most toddlers are delighted when adults exaggerate and turn on the silliness. Grandpa can ham it up…the more preposterous, the better. This is a chance for him to shine.

Toddlers also love repetition. Doing the same thing more than once with Grandpa may become a ritual they look forward to with every visit. Toddlers will request those "only with Grandpa" activities—filling the birdbath, walking to the mailbox, feeding the dog and checking the garden. Grandpa will undoubtedly be glad to grant each wish.

Lynne: Grandpa Bruce had a special tickly kiss on the neck he gave our grandchildren whenever they said goodbye to him. They loved it! It was a giggly treat only Grandpa offered. He even gave out extras as rewards for quickly scrambling into car seats when they headed for home. Worked every time!

Inside the house, Grandpa can:

• GET DOWN ON THE FLOOR and play make-believe with cars and trains. He can start those engines with the special vroom-vroom sound that grandpas do so well.

• INVENT STORIES starring the toddler's favorite teddy bear, doll or puppet. Stretch his grandchild's growing vocabulary with new words.

• PLAY AN INDOOR BALL GAME with soft foam balls. Hand-eye coordination skills take lots of practice.

• PLAY A SIMPLE HIDING GAME Hide a toy and look for it together. Take this game to the next level by giving his grandchild clues as to where the toy is hiding. Can he find it all by himself?

• DANCE WITH HIS GRANDCHILD standing on grandpa's feet so the two of them, holding hands, can walk or move together. Really silly fun!

• SHARE HIS SHOES What child can resist putting on and trying to walk in Grandpa's huge shoes? A good "photo op."

• GIVE PIGGYBACK OR HORSEY RIDES if Grandpa's back can take it. This game is so popular that you may want to set the timer to limit it. Otherwise, the rides might go on and on.

• READ WITH HIS GRANDCHILD, side-by-side on the couch, each with his own reading material or read aloud to her from her favorite book...a great way to show that reading is a pleasure for all ages.

• STRETCH OUT AND NAP TOGETHER...an all-time favorite activity!

Going outside, Grandpa can:

• TURN AN EVERYDAY LUNCH INTO A PICNIC by taking it out to eat in the yard, on the deck or at the park. Fresh air is good for appetites. Bonus: easy clean-up.

• PLAY SIMPLE BALL GAMES Throw, kick, roll and bounce, using easy-to-hold balls designed for young children. Good exercise for all players!

• CARRY HIS GRANDCHILD ON HIS SHOULDERS to give him a different view of the world. What can a child see from up there?

• GO FOR WALKS, EVEN IN THE RAIN Splishing and splashing are perhaps more to Grandpa's liking than to Grammie's. Toddlers love a chance to wear those colorful rubber rain boots, coats and hats.

• BECOME A NATURE GUIDE Help hunt for roly-poly bugs and butterflies or float leaves in puddles.

• VISIT A PET SHOP, FISH STORE OR PETTING ZOO Grandpa can be the first to introduce him to an iguana, piranha or llama.

• **GIVE SLED OR WAGON RIDES** Here is a chance to talk about fast and slow, bumpy and smooth, and stop and go.

• **TAKE HIS GRANDCHILD TO THE PARK** to climb on the jungle gym. Grandpas generally allow more risk-taking than grammies. As long as he keeps a watchful eye, this more relaxed approach can be a good confidence builder for toddlers.

GRANDPA WITH PRESCHOOLERS

Preschoolers often initiate play and would love Grandpa to join them. At this age, they are ready for more structured games, extended projects and ambitious outings.

Inside the house, Grandpa can:

• **PLAY HIDE-AND-SEEK** Preschoolers are more aware of game rules and can count to ten before hunting for Grandpa. Some peeking is to be expected.

• **TEACH CARD GAMES** like Old Maid, Go Fish or Crazy Eights. Reminder: little children find it very hard to lose. Can the rules be bent in their favor now and then?

• **PLAY WITH DOMINOES** Show how to use them as a matching game or as a knock-down chain reaction activity.

• **BRING OUT TINKER TOYS** New generations still appreciate this old classic.

• SPREAD OUT A JIGSAW PUZZLE If this activity catches on, keep at it. Otherwise, save it for later.

• TRY SIMPLE BOARD GAMES What about the old favorites like Hi Ho! Cherry-O or Candy Land, or the newer cooperative games that focus on team effort rather than individual winners and losers?

• GIVE A SHAVING LESSON Squirt a bit of shaving cream on the child's cheek or chin so she can "shave" using a Popsicle stick or tongue depressor as a razor. Just like Grandpa…

• BUILD STRUCTURES with blocks and Legos or construct ramps for racing little cars. Make this as simple or elaborate an activity as time allows. There is no end to the imaginative play with props like toweling tubes, paper and markers, emergency vehicles and miniature figures…perfect for a rainy day.

Getting out of the house, Grandpa can:

• GO SHOPPING and involve his preschooler in a simple purchase. Could the child pass real money to the clerk? This is a good opportunity to teach that actual money buys goods even in this world of overused credit cards.

Cindy: As a child, I spent summers with my grandparents in a small town. My grandfather and I went "over town" each morning to pick up the paper before the rest of the house was awake. While he drove, we talked about the day ahead, the weather and anything else that came to mind. He gave me the nickel, let me buy the paper and showed me off to his friends.

• GET A HAIRCUT with his grandchild watching. If it is OK with the child's parents, can he get one too?

• DRIVE THROUGH THE CAR WASH with the child as a passenger. Then vacuum the interior together and talk about the satisfaction of having a clean car.

• **SHOW HOW TO BE A CREATURE DETECTIVE** Follow ants to find their nest or snail trails to see where they lead. Look for footprints in the mud or snow. Who made these…deer, rabbits, birds or the neighborhood dog?

• **GO ON HIKES OR BIKE RIDES** Choose a destination and then plan together what is needed for a successful outing…helmet, water, sunscreen, snacks and a jacket.

• **VISIT CONSTRUCTION SITES** Preschoolers are old enough to understand the process of building and how machines make the job easier. Go back later to check on the progress.

• **DIG MUD HOLES OR BUILD** sand or mud castles together… a good follow-up to the construction site visit.

• **DRAW A SIMPLE MAP** of the house or yard. Follow the map together as you check off each landmark. Is there an X marking the spot of hidden treasure at the end?

• **BUILD FORTS** in the snow or houses from sheets or boxes…a chance to inspire a budding architect or engineer.

• **FIND A PLACE TO WATCH AIRPLANES** take off and land. What is the difference between a jet and a prop plane?

• **FLY KITES AND MAKE PAPER AIRPLANES** Can Grandpa explain why they stay up in the air?

• **PLAY BALL**…baseball, soccer or basketball. A preschooler can begin to learn the rules of playing and scoring.

 *Cindy:* Grandpa Jim, an avid golfer, came home one day with child-sized putters for our grandsons. Though too young to grasp the fine points of the game, the boys worked seriously on their "technique," aiming at coasters on the floor for their hole-in-one.

• **INVITE A GRANDPA FRIEND AND HIS GRANDCHILD** to come along to a local baseball or football game. Take binoculars and plan to buy popcorn and hotdogs.

• **WORK IN THE GARDEN** and show his little helper how to poke holes and drop in the seeds for new plants. His young gardener can learn to weed and water and can share in the final reward of the harvest.

Laurie: My grandfather's garden was his pride and joy. He'd walk with me through the rows of cornstalks, lettuce, peppers and beans. We picked the ripe vegetables, talking about their different shapes and colors and how we liked to eat them. My older cousin may have been Champion Corn Husker, but I earned the title of Master Bean Snapper!

• **SHARE HIS INTEREST IN MUSIC** Does Grandpa play the piano, harmonica or guitar? Is he willing to give his grandchild a try with it?

• **PERFORM A FEW SIMPLE MAGIC TRICKS** Children this age are easily enchanted. "How did Grandpa do that?"

• **GO BOWLING TOGETHER** Check ahead to see if the local alley will set up bumper bowling for young children.

• **TAKE A STAR WALK AT NIGHT** and point out the constellations. There is a great app for smart phones to help with identification.

• **STAGE A CAMP OUT IN THE BACK YARD** Even if they do not spend the night, it is great fun to pretend to live in the wilderness.

Lynne: I'll never forget the night I discovered my grandsons and Grandpa Bruce at their make-believe campfire. They were sitting cross-legged in our darkened bathroom under the glow of the red heat lamp telling stories. It warmed my heart that my husband could be such a playful grandpa. He had not only turned our bathroom into a pre-bedtime campfire site, but had turned the boys' overnight stay into a real adventure.

Some things never change

Although the playground equipment children climb on and the toys they collect today may look quite different from those of thirty years ago, some things never change. Children still need the encouragement, interest and love of the adults in their lives. Grandfathers, whatever their style or approach, can and will make lasting impressions on their grandchildren.

The infant of today quickly becomes the teenager of tomorrow. Whether Grandpa taught her to play ball as a toddler or "hunt wildlife" with a camera when she was five, that grandchild may look to her grandfather for support and guidance through the years. What an opportunity Grandpa has to start that journey with his grandchild right now!

CHAPTER **10**

YOU MAKE A DIFFERENCE

BEFORE WRITING THIS LAST CHAPTER, WE FOUR FRIENDS reflected on our relationships with our own grandmothers and the impact they had on us. Although each grandmother was very different in style and personality, we found some recurring themes in the roles they played in our lives— chronicling the past, keeping traditions and providing support and perspective in times of challenge. As grammies now ourselves, we wondered if these roles would be part of our legacy and how we would fulfill them.

KEEPING FAMILY HISTORY ALIVE

A grandmother was telling her little granddaughter what her own childhood was like: "We used to skate outside on a pond. I had a swing made from a tire; it hung from a tree in our front yard. We rode our pony. We picked wild raspberries in the woods." The little girl was wide-

eyed, taking this in. At last she said, "I sure wish I'd gotten to know you sooner!"

Grandmothers are the natural historians of the family. They are in fact the link from the past to the present, keeping the family lore alive. Knowledge of unique family history will disappear with the passing of each generation if it is not shared. Here are ways to carry it forward:

• TEACH THE SONGS, EXPRESSIONS, POEMS AND GAMES you remember from childhood.

• IF ANOTHER LANGUAGE IS PART OF YOUR FAMILY'S CULTURE, use some phrases in casual conversations so that your grandchild can hear the language of her heritage. You will be surprised at how many words she will pick up.

• LOOK THROUGH OLD FAMILY PHOTOGRAPHS and talk about places you have lived, adventures you have had or family gatherings through the years. Perhaps there are stories about a great-grandfather who was a railroad engineer or a great-great-grandmother who traveled across the ocean to settle in this country.

• SHARE STORIES ABOUT YOUR GRANDCHILD'S PARENTS Where else will she hear about them as children and begin to see them as people who had to learn and practice, fail and grow?

Jan: I remember asking my mother to "tell me the story" of her life. It was the way I learned about her childhood. Now I tell those tales to my grandchildren and they ask for stories about me. I've started to write them down because I realize their value to the family.

• ORGANIZE FAMILY PHOTOGRAPHS Scrapbooking magazines and websites give suggestions for putting your family history into a form that will be kept for years. Or take advantage of the internet for creating albums that can be available to family members when they are online. Numerous photograph websites will guide you through the process.

TIP: To rescue and preserve old photographs, movies or videos, check out archiving services. Google such terms as "preserving photos" or "preserving videos." Most archivists recommend saving material in at least two formats because technology is constantly updated.

• DRAW A FAMILY TREE to help your grandchildren visualize where different family members fit in the overall scheme. Preschoolers will delight in seeing their names alongside Grandpa Joe and Cousin Caitlin. This can help them understand that Aunt Sarah is her Mommy's sister and why Uncle Bill looks so much like Grandpa Joe.

CARRYING ON TRADITIONS

Every family has its valued customs. The more established ones often revolve around seasons, ethnic and religious holidays and special occasions. The food that is served, the way the house is decorated, the music that is played at these times...some of these are traditions that have endured for several generations and grammies are usually the ones to carry them forward.

There are also many traditions you can create on your own that are simple, perhaps unintentional, but equally meaningful. Something you have done with your grandchildren only two or three times may become what they look forward to again and again.

• POPCORN FOR SUPPER ON SUNDAY NIGHTS

• CLINKING GLASSES AND SAYING "CHEERS" AT MEALTIME

• WATERING THE POTTED PLANTS AT EVERY VISIT

• BUTTERFLY KISSES WHEN THEY SAY GOOD-BYE

PROVIDING SUPPORT

A grammie has the advantage of perspective gained over the years. You know that many of the concerns parents lose sleep over today will evaporate with time. There is wisdom in the phrase: "This too shall pass."

Some of the frustrating behaviors of childhood translate into strengths in an adult. Many grammies have seen it happen: the single-minded toddler becomes the teen who avoids distractions and remains focused on his goals; the child who was always reluctant to participate becomes the keen observer and peacemaker in society; the strong-willed four-year-old becomes an effective adult leader; the child who said "no" so vehemently to his parents is later able to say "no" to temptations in life.

Entire families may face struggles, too—illness, divorce, financial strain. Grammie may be the anchor during rocky times…the person to whom both her children and grandchildren can turn for stability and emotional support. Your faith in the future, your steadiness, your continued love will go a long way toward helping them get through these tough times. Many grammies may be remembered not so much for their sparkling personalities but for their strength, endurance and ability to cope in the midst of stress.

YOUR GIFT OF TIME

Spoil your grandchild not with gifts but with attention. —Linda Sunshine

Certainly grammies who offer support and maintain family history and traditions leave a legacy that will be valued by grandchildren in later years. But what about the special gifts you can give your young grandchildren here and now that can make a difference in their lives?

In this hurry-up world with all its distractions, your unhurried time and undivided attention are special gifts you can offer. Turn off the television, let voicemail take the phone calls and set aside time just for your grandchild. If you really want to make her feel important, ask her what SHE would like to do today...and, if possible, go do it.

A hand to hold

We should all have one person who knows how to bless us despite the evidence. Grandmother was that person to me. —Phyllis Theroux

When a child struggles, she needs to know someone is in her corner. You can be your young grandchild's safe haven, offering a hug or a lap to sit on. With careful listening, you may be able to understand what the upset is really all about. You can let a little one know she has been heard and give her the time to recoup until she is ready to move on.

 Cindy: In my childhood my grandmother was often away from home so I spent more time with Granddad. When I was upset, he knew how to comfort me. He stopped what he was doing, listened to my troubles and could always put a smile back on my face.

MEMORIES

What comes to mind when you think of your own grandmother? Perhaps from your childhood memories you recall the way she greeted you at the door, her collection of figurines, the aroma of her freshly baked apple pie, her insistence on good table manners. Now as an adult you may think of her more in terms of her personality and interests. Maybe she was...

• A HOMEMAKER who kept a clean and welcoming home and had a solution for every household mishap.

• A TRAVELER who shared her adventures in faraway places.

• A WOMAN OF FAITH who set an example of worship.

- ONE WHO APPRECIATED THE FINE ARTS and introduced you to music and museums.

- A LOVER OF NATURE who led you on discovery walks through the woods.

- A WOMAN WHO SEEMED TO PREFER ADULT COMPANY to yours.

- AN AVID READER with stacks of books by her bed and a new library book for you every time you visited.

- A KITCHEN MAGICIAN who taught you how to make that perfect gravy.

- SOMEONE WHO ALWAYS LOOKED ON THE BRIGHT SIDE and truly believed that life is worth living.

- AN ARTIST AT HEART who had a flair for decorating her home, for painting or for stitchery.

- A SPORTSWOMAN who shared her love of the game.

- A QUIET PERSON who was content to let others take the stage.

- A SILLY AND PLAYFUL FRIEND who remembered how to giggle in the dark, tell a knock-knock joke and dance in the rain.

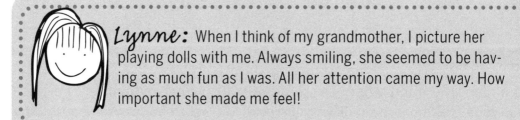

Lynne: When I think of my grandmother, I picture her playing dolls with me. Always smiling, she seemed to be having as much fun as I was. All her attention came my way. How important she made me feel!

Your young grandchild's memories of you begin now with the simple things he observes about you. Each time you are together his picture of you becomes more complete. He notices the way you look, the sound of your voice and what you like to do. As he matures he will fill in the picture even more, as you did with your grandmother.

Expose your grandchild to what has been important to you—your values and life's lessons. You can be an important figure in his childhood and an influence on who he becomes as an adult. Here is a glimpse into some of the ways we four grammies have shared with our grandchildren what we care about and who we are.

Laurie: I come from a big family and it was important to me that my children and their children feel strongly connected to our relatives and to my roots on the east coast. Yet I ended up raising my children in the West...far from where I grew up and where my folks still lived. To maintain ties with our extended family and my heritage, I resolved to visit my girlhood home at least once a year. From the time my first child was only 5-weeks-old, we climbed on a plane for our annual cross country journey. It was during those summer days on the coast of Maine that we established our most cherished and continuing traditions.

Even now with my grandchildren we gather to explore tide pools, splash on the shore, dig for clams, eat lobster, row the boat to "our" deserted island, build fairy houses in the woods and play in our four-generational baseball games. From year to year I add photographs to the album of our Summers in Maine. The background scenes are always the same but we all appreciate the record of how the players captured in those photographs have grown and multiplied.

Jan: I am a nature lover. I try to share that passion with my grandchildren through gardening, outdoor discoveries and exploration. No one was surprised then when I introduced and fostered the "Hairy the Pumpkin" project. He is now an established part of our fall festivities.

After Halloween each year we take a good-sized jack-o'-lantern and stuff it with strips of wet newspaper. Just ripping up the newspaper, dumping the strips in a bucket of water and squeezing them out before filling the pumpkin is great fun. Then we sprinkle soaked soft wheat berries on the top opening and also into the eyes, nose, mouth and ear cut-outs.

We set the pumpkin outside on a tray or in the garden and keep it well watered. In a week the seeds begin sprouting to make green grassy hair—not only on the top of its head but from eyes, ears, nose and mouth. Once begun, this "hair" grows quickly and may continue growing for a month or two depending on the outdoor temperature. He becomes a very hairy, funny fellow—thus the name "Hairy the Pumpkin."

My grandchildren drew pictures showing how he had changed from week to week, eventually going back to the earth. "Hairy gave his all for the garden," we declared.

Want to try it? Check the details in the Appendix.

Cindy: The times I treasure most in my life as a grandmother are those when my entire family is together. I love getting us organized for whatever we are going to do that day. It could be a hike in the woods in the morning, a trip to the park in the afternoon or a game around the dining room table after dinner; but, rest assured, we are going to be active and it is going to include all three generations.

Having our family with us at holiday time brought the chance to enjoy fun-filled activities that have become favorite family traditions and only get better with each new year. When our grandchildren were still under five years old, we began to hold the Thanksgiving Olympics—a hit from the very first year.

We started with simple contests using familiar toys: a bowling set, soccer ball, basketball, baseball, a bucket and apples for bobbing. It was the adults versus the kids and each event was short, one or two tries per person. As the children got older we expanded the contests and made them a little more difficult. We even added a touch football game because our family was so into sports.

During the first years the grown-ups held back a bit to let the grandchildren win. But it didn't take long before we were trying as hard as we could. I made special T-shirts every year for each team member and it was a BIG deal as I introduced my grandchildren one-by-one to the Old Folks Team. Trophies for the winners? No need, each athlete was thrilled with a Tootsie Pop as the prize!

Lynne: For me, being able to spend time with a grandchild is one of life's greatest blessings. We don't need to go anywhere special or do anything monumental. Just being together, chatting, playing, cooking, singing, reading, exploring, laughing... these are the sweetest moments of being a grandmother.

"Tuesdays at Grandma's" began when our oldest grandson was only a few months old so I could capture an entire day with the baby. It has become a weekly tradition ever since, one that both my grandchildren and I treasure.

As siblings arrived, they were welcomed to the rotation, each child having his special "Tuesday" in turn. On that day we read the books or get out the toys he selects, take field trips to places that fit his particular interests and do the activities he chooses, often including Grandpa. By focusing on a single grandchild for an entire day, I have come to appreciate and love each one and his uniqueness far more completely than if my attention were divided among all four boys. Each grandchild, in turn, basks in a grown-up's full attention for the day (which in a house full of four active, healthy young boys is a near impossibility for any parent to provide).

At the end of a "Tuesday" I briefly journal what we did, the cute things our special guest said and may attach a photograph or sample of his artwork. Occasionally the older boys and I take a peek at those memory pages together and just chuckle about what great "Tuesdays" we've shared. I so wish my grandchildren who live far away could be part of this tradition too.

WHAT'S IN STORE FOR YOU

There is no way to know for sure how your grandchild will remember you or how the things you are saying or doing with him will eventually impact his life. You can only be true to your own nature and individual style. Many things will contribute to your legacy, such as your personality and that of your grandchild, your interests and his, your energy level and his and the amount of time you can spend together. There is no one right way.

Will there be surprises? Yes!

• **CHILDREN CAN BE A CHALLENGE IN THE EATING DEPARTMENT** One grandchild loves broccoli; another turns up her nose and pushes the serving aside. We learned that apparently it does matter how sandwiches are presented—with crust or without, cut in triangles or squares.

• **CHILDREN CAN BE BRUTALLY HONEST AND YOUR VANITY WILL BE TESTED** "Why do you have 'lines' on your face?" "How come you have wobbly arms?" "Why can't you run as fast as I can?" Take a deep breath and keep your sense of humor.

• **CHILDREN CAN STUMP YOU WITH THEIR QUESTIONS** How do you answer when they ask: "Why did they make three come after two?" "Where does the universe stop?" "Is there a heaven just for goldfish?" Hmmm, food for thought.

• **WHAT WORKED WITH YOUR OWN CHILDREN MAY NOT WORK WITH YOUR GRANDCHILDREN** Children today are generally more outspoken and not as quick to follow directions.

• **CHILDREN CAN BE GREAT TEACHERS** They remind us how much fun it is to play again—to squish play dough, dig in the sand, dress a doll or play catch.

• **BEING AROUND YOUNG CHILDREN IS A REMINDER OF THE RELENTLESSNESS OF PARENTING** There are no breaks. We may not always admit it, but there are times when the peace and quiet after our grandchildren leave is welcome.

• **GRANDCHILDREN LOVE US ALMOST WITHOUT ANY EFFORT ON OUR PART**...there is a natural attraction of grandchildren for their grandparents.

• **FALLING IN LOVE WITH A GRANDCHILD HAPPENS VERY QUICKLY—** even for a woman who thinks she is a little too young or that her life is too busy to be a grandmother. Her reservations disappear as soon as she holds that first grandchild.

Will there be laughs? Many!

Art Linkletter was right…"kids say the darndest things." As they struggle to increase their vocabulary and express their thoughts, you will chuckle as you hear such phrases as:

• "SEE, GRANDMA. I REMEMBERED TO USE MY 'LAPKIN' TO WIPE MY HANDS."

• "I WANT TO BE A BALLET-ER WHEN I GROW UP OR MAYBE A LEMONADE STAND-ER."

• WHEN A BALL GOES OFF THE FIELD OF PLAY, IT GOES "OUT OF BOUNCE."

• "TO STOP MY SNIFFLES, I NEED A BAND-AID FOR MY NOSE."

• "LET'S SING THAT SONG ABOUT RUDOLPH THE RED-NOSED PRAYIN' DEER."

• "I LIKE THOSE 'CHEESE LEADERS' AT THE GAME WITH THEIR POM-POMS."

• "THERE'S A "BACK GO" TRUCK OVER THERE! SEE THE SCOOPER PULLING UP THE DIRT?"

• A CHURCH CHRISTENING WITH LOTS OF WATER IS A "BATH-TISM."

• WHILE LOOKING AT GOLDFISH IN A TANK, A GRANDCHILD SAID, "ALL THOSE FISH HAVE ON THE SAME CLOTHES."

Our list could go on and on. You will have no trouble collecting quips from your own grandchildren. Be sure to write them down.

The flip side

I know now that being a grandmother is what fills your heart with love and your soul with meaning. —Thirza Beck Devlin

Although this last chapter has focused on the impact we can have on our grandchildren, we now clearly see how much we have been changed by them. This is the flip side of grandparenting.

The arrival of grandchildren has added a new dimension to our lives, giving us a renewed sense of purpose. When they are near, we feel younger, perhaps, and re-energized. They nudge us out of our comfort zone, asking us to be playful and spontaneous and reminding us that relationships are what matter most in life. This is their gift to us.

Our grandchildren have enhanced our lives beyond measure. Because of them we live more fully, laugh more often and love more completely.

APPENDIX

Recipes for Crafts

PLAY DOUGH #1

½ cup salt

1 cup flour

1 teaspoon cream of tartar

1 tablespoon oil

1 cup water

½ teaspoon food coloring

(Add to water before combining with other ingredients. Adding a drop of lemon or peppermint extract makes a lovely-smelling play dough.)

Mix ingredients in saucepan. Cook over medium heat, stirring constantly until dough thickens and can be stirred into a ball. Remove from heat and continue stirring about a minute. Turn hot ball onto a floured surface. Knead with floured hands until it cools enough to play with. Store in a resealable plastic bag or tightly closed container. It lasts for weeks.

This recipe is also used for modeling clay. Objects left to air-dry until hard can be painted or sprayed with acrylic sealer.

PLAY DOUGH #2

1 cup flour

½ cup salt

1 cup water

1 tablespoon oil

2 teaspoons cream of tartar

1 small package (3-½ ounce) sugar free Jell-O

Mix all ingredients together and cook over medium heat, stirring constantly until the consistency of mashed potatoes. Cool a few minutes and then knead with floured hands until the mixture no longer sticks to your hands. Smells yummy!

GOOP

Here is another recipe for more finger fun.

Cornstarch

Water

Tray or bowl

Spoons

Food coloring (optional)

Mix 1 cup cornstarch with 1/2 cup (colored) water. Pour this mixture onto a tray or into a shallow bowl. Stir with fingers or spoon. Add more cornstarch. What happens? Stir and add more water. How does the goop feel now? This is a totally tactile experience. Bet Grammie can't resist squeezing it too.

Tip: Have lots of cornstarch on hand, and be ready to squish and squeeze the mixture for a long time! May be saved and reused for a number of days—simply add a little water to reconstitute it.

Projects for Watching Things Grow

HAIRY THE PUMPKIN

A good-sized pumpkin carved into a jack-o'-lantern

Shredded or torn strips of newspaper

Water

Soft wheat berries, soaked overnight to accelerate sprouting. (Soft wheat berries are available at health food stores or some grocery stores.)

Soak the shredded newspaper in water and then stuff the carved pumpkin with the paper, filling it to the brim. Sprinkle the wheat berries liberally on the top, and push some into the eye, ear, mouth, and nose openings. Place in your garden or on a tray outside and water daily. A spray bottle or watering can works well.

The wheat berries will begin to sprout grass in about three days. Within ten days or so, the pumpkin will have "hair" sprouting on his head, out his eyes, nose, mouth and ears—thus becoming "Hairy, the Pumpkin," a funny-looking fellow. As the grass grows, Hairy shrivels and returns to the earth, demonstrating how Mother Nature recycles.

Tip: If you live where winter comes early, create your "Hairy" as soon as you are able to purchase pumpkins in the fall.

A SPRING BASKET

Here is another use for wheat berries.

A small basket

Foil or plastic wrap

Paper towels

Soft wheat berries, soaked overnight

Line the basket with foil or plastic wrap. Place wet paper towels over the lining and sprinkle with the soft wheat berries. Keep moist. In about three days the grass will sprout. Watch to see how tall it will grow. Could your grandchild give it a haircut with safety scissors? Trimmed or not, this can be part of your spring table centerpiece.

Songs, Rhymes and Finger Plays
(listed in alphabetical order)

ALPHABET SONG

(to the same tune as *Twinkle, Twinkle, Little Star*)

A,b,c,d,e,f,g,

H,i,j,k,l,m,n,o,p,

Q,r,s,t,u,v,

W,x,y and z.

Now I know my ABC's

Next time won't you sing with me?

APPLE TREE, ORANGE TREE, LEMON TREE

WORDS	ACTIONS
Way up high in the apple tree	Reach up high with both arms.
Ten little apples smiled down at me.	Smile.
I shook that tree just as hard as I could.	"Shake" a tree.
Down fell the apples.	Bring arms down like falling.
M-m-m they were good!	Rub tummy.
Repeat with oranges.	
Repeat with a lemon tree but change the last line to: *Oooooooh, they were sour!*	Squint eyes and squeeze lips, like tasting a sour lemon.

ARE YOU SLEEPING?

Are you sleeping,

Are you sleeping,

Brother John? Brother John?

Morning bells are ringing.
Morning bells are ringing.

Ding, ding, dong.
Ding, ding, dong.

A TISKET, A TASKET

A tisket, a tasket

A green and yellow basket.

I wrote a letter to my love

And on the way I dropped it.

I dropped it, I dropped it

And on the way I dropped it.

A little boy (girl) picked it up

And put it in his (her) pocket.

BAA, BAA, BLACK SHEEP

Baa, baa, black sheep, have you any wool?

Yes sir, yes sir, three bags full.

One for my master and one for my dame.

And one for the little boy who lives down the lane.

Baa, baa, black sheep, have you any wool?

Yes sir, yes sir, three bags full.

THE BEAR WENT OVER THE MOUNTAIN

Oh, the bear went over the mountain,

The bear went over the mountain,

The bear went over the mountain

To see what he could see.

The other side of the mountain,

The other side of the mountain,

The other side of the mountain,

Was all that he could see.

BIRTHDAY FINGER PLAY

WORDS	ACTIONS
Today is _____'s birthday. Let's make him (her) a cake.	Fill in your grandchild's name.
Stir and mix, mix and stir,	Use stirring action.
Then into the oven to bake.	Pretend to put in an oven.
Here's our cake so nice and round.	Make round circle with your arms.
Let's frost it pink (or blue) and white	Make frosting motion.
Now we'll put (number of birthdays) candles on it to make a birthday light.	Count candles while you pretend to stick them in the cake. Then blow them out.

EENSY, WEENSY SPIDER

WORDS	ACTIONS
The eensy, weensy spider climbed up the water spout,	March your fingers up your arm or touch each index finger to the thumb of your other hand and twist your wrists to resemble a climbing motion.
Down came the rain and washed the spider out.	Arms up high and lower them as you wiggle your fingers.
Out came the sun and dried up all the rain and	Make a big circle above your head with your arms.
The eensy, weensy spider climbed up the spout again.	Repeat the climbing motion.

THE FARMER IN THE DELL

The farmer in the dell.

The farmer in the dell.

Hi-Ho, the derry-o!

The farmer in the dell

The farmer takes a wife.

The farmer takes a wife.

Hi-Ho, the derry-o!

The farmer takes a wife.

The wife takes a child.

The wife takes a child.

Hi-Ho, the derry-o!

The wife takes a child.

Succeeding verses:

The child takes a nurse, etc.

The nurse takes a cat, etc.

The cat takes a rat, etc.

The rat takes the cheese, etc.

The cheese stands alone, etc.

FIVE LITTLE MONKEYS

WORDS	ACTIONS
Five little monkeys jumping on the bed.	Bounce hand with all five fingers spread.
One fell off and bumped his head.	Pat the top of your head.
Mama called the doctor and the doctor said,	Pretend to hold a phone.
"No more monkeys jumping on the bed!"	Shake your index finger as if scolding.
Four little monkeys...three little monkeys...two little monkeys...one little monkey...	Continue as a countdown showing one less finger each time until...
No more monkeys jumping on the bed!	

THE GRAND OLD DUKE OF YORK

The Grand Old Duke of York,

He had ten thousand men;

He marched them up to the top of the hill,

And marched them down again.

And when you're up they're up.

And when you're down they're down.

And when you're only halfway up,

You're neither up nor down.

HERE IS A BUNNY

WORDS	ACTIONS
Here is a bunny with ears so funny	Hold up two fingers on one hand and wiggle them.
And here is a hole in the ground.	Make a circle with the index finger and thumb of your other hand.
When a noise he hears, he pricks up his ears	Straighten up your two "bunny" fingers,
And jumps in the hole in the ground.	And then quickly hop the fingers into the hole made by your other hand.

HERE IS THE CHURCH

WORDS	ACTIONS
Here is the church.	Fingers of both hands intertwined and hidden in your palms.
Here is the steeple.	Index fingers pop up, pointed together to shape the steeple.
Open the doors,	Thumbs part.
And see all the people.	Intertwined fingers pop up, hands are back to back and fingers wiggle.

HERE WE GO 'ROUND THE MULBERRY BUSH

Here we go round the mulberry bush,

The mulberry bush,

The mulberry bush.

Here we go round the mulberry bush

On a cold and frosty morning.

This is the way we wash our clothes,

Wash our clothes, wash our clothes.

This is the way we wash our clothes

On a cold and frosty morning.

(continue with tasks)

This is the way...

We iron our clothes.

Wash our face.

Brush our teeth.

Put on our clothes, etc.

HICKORY DICKORY DOCK

WORDS	ACTIONS
Hickory dickory dock, the mouse ran up the clock.	Walk fingers up arm.
The clock struck one,	Clap once.
The mouse ran down, Hickory dickory dock.	Walk fingers down arm.

HUMPTY DUMPTY

Humpty Dumpty sat on a wall.

Humpty Dumpty had a great fall.

All the king's horses and all the king's men

Couldn't put Humpty together again.

I'VE BEEN WORKING ON THE RAILROAD

I've been working on the railroad all the livelong day.

I've been working on the railroad just to pass the time away.

Can't you hear the whistle blowing? Rise up so early in the morn.

Can't you hear the captain shouting, "Dinah, blow your horn!"

JACK AND JILL

Jack and Jill went up the hill to fetch a pail of water.

Jack fell down and broke his crown,

And Jill came tumbling after.

JACK BE NIMBLE

Jack be nimble.

Jack be quick.

Jack jump over

The candlestick.

JINGLE BELLS

Jingle bells, jingle bells, jingle all the way,

Oh, what fun it is to ride in a one-horse, open sleigh.

Repeat...

JOHN JACOB JINGLEHEIMER SCHMIDT

John Jacob Jingleheimer Schmidt, his name is my name too.

Whenever we go out, the people always shout,

"There goes John Jacob

Jingleheimer Schmidt,

Da-da-da-da-da-da-dah!"

Repeat...

LITTLE BOY BLUE

Little Boy Blue, come blow your horn

The sheep's in the meadow, the cow's in the corn;

But where is the boy who looks after the sheep?

He's under the haystack, fast asleep.

LITTLE MISS MUFFETT

Little Miss Muffet sat on a tuffett,

Eating her curds and whey;

Along came a spider who sat down beside her

And frightened Miss Muffett away.

LONDON BRIDGE IS FALLING DOWN

London Bridge is falling down,

Falling down, falling down.

London Bridge is falling down.

My fair lady.

Take the key and lock her up,

Lock her up, lock her up.

Take the key and lock her up.

My fair lady.

MARY HAD A LITTLE LAMB

Mary had a little lamb, little lamb, little lamb,

Mary had a little lamb; its fleece was white as snow.

And everywhere that Mary went, Mary went, Mary went,

Everywhere that Mary went, the lamb was sure to go.

It followed her to school one day, school one day, school one day,

It followed her to school one day which was against the rules.

It made the children laugh and play, laugh and play, laugh and play.

It made the children laugh and play to see a lamb at school.

And so the teacher turned it out, turned it out, turned it out.

And so the teacher turned it out but still it lingered near.

And waited patiently about, -ly about, -ly about

And waited patiently about till Mary did appear.

"Why does the lamb love Mary so, Mary so, Mary so.

Why does the lamb love Mary so?" the eager children cry.

"Why Mary loves the lamb you know, the lamb you know, the lamb you know.

Why Mary loves the lamb you know," the Teacher did reply.

MOUSIE

WORDS	ACTIONS
Mousie, Mousie, Mousie, Mousie, *Coming up to Baby's housie!*	Walk index finger and middle finger up baby's arm toward her face and tickle her under the chin. You can use this, too, to encourage eating by holding a spoonful of food as you go.
Here's a little Mousie coming up the stairs, Looking for a warm place. Oops! Right there!	Walk index finger and middle finger up baby's body. Then with the Oops, quickly tuck fingers under her chin or under her arm!

OLD MACDONALD HAD A FARM

Old MacDonald had a farm, E-I-E-I-O

And on that farm he had a pig (or cow or duck or...), E-I-E-I-O

With an oink, oink here, and an oink, oink there,

Here an oink, there an oink, everywhere an oink, oink,

Old MacDonald had a farm, E-I-E-I-O.

ONE, TWO, BUCKLE MY SHOE

One, two buckle my shoe,

three-four shut the door,

five-six pick up sticks,

seven-eight lay them straight,

nine-ten a big fat hen,

That was fun, let's do it again!

OPEN, SHUT THEM

WORDS	ACTIONS
Open, shut them. Open, shut them.	Open and shut your hands, etc.
Give a little clap.	Motions follow the words.
Open, shut them. Open, shut them.	
Put them in your lap.	
Creeping, crawling, creeping, crawling, right up to your chin.	Creep fingers slowly from tummy to chin.
Open up your little mouth.	Open your mouth.
But do not let them in.	Quickly hide your hands behind your back.

PETER POUNDS WITH ONE HAMMER
(TO THE TUNE OF DID YOU EVER SEE A LASSIE?)

WORDS	ACTIONS
Peter pounds with one hammer, one hammer, one hammer. Peter pounds with one hammer, one hammer, one.	Pound one fist on knee in rhythm.
Peter pounds with two hammers, two hammers, two hammers. Peter pounds with two hammers, two hammers, two.	Pound two fists on knees.
Add three, four and five hammers…	Pound two fists and tap one foot, then two fists and two feet, then two fists and feet and nod head.
Then he goes to sleep.	Slow down and pretend to go to sleep.

POLLY PUT THE KETTLE ON

Polly put the kettle on,

Kettle on, kettle on.

Polly put the kettle on,

We'll all have tea.

POP! GOES THE WEASEL

All around the cobbler's bench

The monkey chased the weasel.

The monkey thought t'was all in fun

Pop! Goes the weasel.

RING AROUND THE ROSIE

Ring around the rosie

Pocket full of posie

Ashes, ashes, we all fall down.

Cows in the meadow

Eating buttercups

Ashes, ashes we all jump up.

ROCK-A-BYE BABY

Rock-a-bye baby, in the treetop

When the wind blows,

The cradle will rock,

When the bough breaks,

The cradle will fall,

And down will come baby,

Cradle and all.

ROW, ROW, ROW YOUR BOAT

Row, row, row your boat gently down the stream.

Merrily, merrily, merrily, merrily, life is but a dream.

SCARY EYES

WORDS	ACTIONS
See my great big scary eyes?	Circle thumb and index fingers around your eyes.
Get ready for a big surprise…BOO!	Pull hands away…and shout BOO!

SHE'LL BE COMING 'ROUND THE MOUNTAIN

She'll be coming 'round the mountain when she comes.

She'll be coming 'round the mountain when she comes.

She'll be coming 'round the mountain; she'll be coming 'round the mountain,

She'll be coming 'round the mountain when she comes.

She'll be driving six white horses when she comes...

We'll all go out to meet her when she comes...

She'll be wearing pink pajamas when she comes...

She'll have to sleep with Grandma when she comes...

We'll all have chicken and dumplings when she comes... etc.

SKIP TO MY LOU

Skip, skip, skip to my Lou,

Skip, skip, skip to my Lou,

Skip, skip, skip to my Lou,

Skip to my Lou, my darling.

THERE WAS A LITTLE TURTLE

WORDS	ACTIONS
There was a little turtle, *He lived in a box.*	Cup both palms, one on top of the other.
He swam in a puddle,	Make a swimming motion.
He climbed on the rocks.	Wiggle your fingers as if you were crawling.
He snapped at a mosquito, *He snapped at a flea.* *He snapped at a minnow,* *He snapped at me.*	Snap thumb and fingers together with "snapped" as the cue.
He caught the mosquito, *He caught the flea.* *He caught the minnow,*	Clap hands together with "caught" as the cue.
But...he didn't catch me!	Shake your head and point to chest.

THIS LITTLE PIGGY

WORDS	ACTIONS
This little piggy went to market.	Wiggle baby's biggest toe.
This little piggy stayed home.	Wiggle second largest toe.
This little piggy had roast beef.	Wiggle third toe.
This little piggy had none.	Wiggle fourth toe.
This little piggy cried, "Whee, whee, whee, whee," *All the way home!*	Wiggle the baby toe, and then tickle the bottom of baby's foot.

THIS OLD MAN

This old man, he played one, he played knick knack on my thumb.

With a knick knack paddy whack, give the dog a bone, this old man came rolling home.

This old man, he played two, he played knick knack on my shoe...

This old man, he played three, he played knick knack on my knee...

This old man, he played four, he played knick knack on my door...

This old man, he played five, he played knick knack on my hive...

TWINKLE, TWINKLE, LITTLE STAR

WORDS	ACTIONS
Twinkle, twinkle, little star,	Use a piano playing motion in front of your torso.
How I wonder what you are.	Point finger at temple as if thinking.
Up above the world so high,	Raise both arms above your head; continue wiggling fingers.
Like a diamond in the sky.	Press both thumbs and index fingers together to make a diamond shape in the air.
Twinkle, twinkle, little star,	Use a piano playing motion in front of your torso.
How I wonder what you are!	Point finger at temple as if thinking.

TWO LITTLE BLACKBIRDS

WORDS	ACTIONS
Two little blackbirds sitting on a hill, one named Jack, the other named Jill.	Hold up index fingers on each hand. Wiggle one for Jack and the other for Jill.
Fly away Jack. Fly away Jill. *Come back, Jack. Come back, Jill.*	Hide one at a time behind your back. Then bring them back one at a time.

WHEELS ON THE BUS

The wheels on the bus go 'round and 'round

(rotate hands around each other)

Round and 'round, 'round and 'round

The wheels on the bus go 'round and 'round,

All over town.

Add your own motions to these additional verses:

The doors on the bus open and shut

The windows on the bus go up and down

The money on the bus goes clink, clink, clink

The driver on the bus says, "Move on back"

The baby on the bus says, "Boo, hoo, hoo"

The Mommy on the bus says, "Shh-shh-shh"

The wipers on the bus go swish, swish, swish

The people on the bus bounce up and down

WHERE IS THUMBKIN?

WORDS	ACTIONS
Where is Thumbkin? Where is Thumbkin?	Begin with both hands in fists behind your back. As you ask the questions, bring your fists out, one by one.
Here I am. Here I am.	Stick up your thumbs, one at a time as you sing the phrases.
How are you today, sir?	Bend one thumb up and down.
Very well, I thank you.	Then bend the other as if to answer.
Run away. Run away.	Put your fists back behind your back, one at a time.

Add verses for fingers: **Pointer, Tall Man, Ring Man and Pinkie.**

WHO'S THERE?

WORDS	ACTIONS
Knock at the door,	Lightly rap with knuckles on your own forehead. (Next time tap on hers.)
Peek in.	Lift one eyelid way wide with index finger.
Pull up the latch,	Use index finger to push tip of nose up toward forehead.
Walk in.	Open mouth wide and insert index finger.

YANKEE DOODLE

Yankee Doodle went to town, a-riding on a pony.

He stuck a feather in his cap, and called it macaroni.

Yankee Doodle keep it up, Yankee Doodle Dandy.

Mind the music and the step and with the girls be handy.

EMERGENCY AUTHORIZATION FORM

Child's Name _____

Birth Date _____

Home Address _____

Phone _____

Father's Name: _____ Mother's Name: _____

Father's Work Phone: _____

Mother's Work Phone: _____

Father's Cell Phone: _____

Mother's Cell Phone: _____

Emergency Contact

Local Relative/friend: _____

Phone: _____

Doctor: _____ Phone: _____

Address: _____

Medical Chart# _____

Dentist: _____ Phone: _____

Address: _____

Insurance Carrier: ID# _____

Medical Advisories

Date of Last Tetanus: _____

Drug allergies: _____

Other: _____

I hereby authorize _____ to secure medical, hospital or dental care for my child(ren), _____, in the event of injury or illness while the child is (children are) in their care. I understand that every effort will be made to contact me before treatment is administered and that I am financially responsible for any care given.

Signature of Parent: _____

Date: _____

RESOURCES

Internet sites change frequently. When seeking information on a topic, be as specific as possible. For example, search "first aid for bee stings," "costumes for preschoolers" or "toilet training."

ART

www.brightring.com
Site includes art activity books by MaryAnn F. Kohl

www.discountschoolsupply.com
Art supplies as well as toys and furniture for young children

www.familyfun.com / magazine
Ideas for crafts

CHILD DEVELOPMENT, HEALTH AND SAFETY

Aamodt, Sandra, Ph.D. and Wang, Sam, Ph.D. *Welcome to Your Child's Brain,* Bloomsbury, USA, 2011.
Current research and practical advice for helping a child reach his potential

Alliance for Childhood
www.allianceforchildhood.com
Advocates the importance of play; offers links to current news articles

American Academy of Pediatrics

> *Caring for Your Baby and Young Child,* Bantam Books, 1998. Advice on medical and parenting questions

> *www.aap.org*
> Developmental topics including limiting screen time

> *www.healthychildren.org*
> Up-to-the-minute pediatric health information and car seat advice

American Association of Retired Persons
www.aarp.org / family / grandparenting
Informational source for grandparents raising children

American Automobile Association
www.aaa.com / carseats
Car seat installation instructions; Safety ranking of baby equipment

Ames, Louise Bates, Ph.D. and Ilg, Frances L, M.D., of the Gesell Institute of Human Development. *Your One-Year-Old,* Dell Publishing, 1982.
First of ten books examining development year by year

Borba, Michele, Ed.D.
www.micheleborba.com
Parenting expert whose books focus on solutions for behavioral problems

Carstensen, Laura, Ph.D. *A Long Bright Future,* Public Affairs, 2011.
Stresses value of grandparenting, in lives of both child and grandparent

Center for Disease Control
www.cdc.gov
A quick reference site for information on childhood health and safety

Christakis, Dimitri, M. *The Elephant in the Room: Make Television Work for Your Kids,* Rodale Books, 2006.

www.commercialfreechildhood.org
Current research on commercialism directed at children

Consumer Product Safety Commission
www.cpsc.gov/cribs
Updates on standards for crib safety and toy recalls

Dancy, Rahima Baldwin. *You Are Your Child's First Teacher,* Celestial Arts, 2000.
Helpful resource for new parents

Elkind, David, Ph.D. *The Hurried Child,* Addison-Wesley Publishing Co, 1982.
Pressures children face when forced to grow up too fast

> *The Power of Play,* Da Capo Press, 2007.
> Well-researched account of the value of creative play

Faber, Adele and Mazlish, Elaine. *How to Talk so Kids Will Listen and Listen so Kids Will Talk,* Scribner, 2012.
Concrete, innovative ways to improve communication with children

Foundation for Grandparenting , Arthur Kornhaber, M.D., Founder/ President
www.grandparenting.org
Promotes healthy relationships between grandparents and grandchildren

Healy, Jane, Ph.D. *Your Child's Growing Mind,* Broadway Books, 2004.
Problems children face when pushed to succeed

Keyser, Janet and David, Laura. *Becoming the Parent You Want to Be,* Broadway Books, 1997.
Practical parenting strategies to handle situations with children to age five

Konner, Melvin. *The Evolution of Childhood,* Belknap Press, 2010.
Presentation of studies on child development by noted anthropologist

Linn, Susan, Ph.D., *The Case for Make-Believe,* The New Press, 2008.
Importance of play and dangers of media and commercialism for young children

National Association for Sports and Physical Education
www.aahperd.org/naspe
Physical activity guidelines for children

Nelson, Jane, Ed.D., Erwin, Sheryl, M.A., and Duffy, Roselyn. *Positive Discipline for Preschoolers,* Three Rivers Press, 1998.
Positive strategies for handling the challenges of raising children

Peck, Betty, Ed.D. *Kindergarten Education: Freeing Children's Creative Potential,* Hawthorn Press, 2004., *A Kindergarten Teacher Looks at the Word GOD: Reflections on Goodness, Oneness and Diversity,* Rudolf Steiner College Press, 2008

ACTIVITIES TO STIMULATE CREATIVITY AND IMAGINATION

Schmitt, Barton D., M.D., F.A.A.P. *Your Child's Health,* Bantam Books, 2005.
Guide to health questions and behavior problems of children from birth to 12

Talaris Institute
www.talaris.org
Current research with video tips for raising emotionally healthy children

www.travel.state.gov
Regulations for traveling with minors

LITERATURE AND LANGUAGE

www.abebooks.com
Used and out-of-print books

www.babysignlanguage.com
Sign language for pre-verbal children

www.childrensbooks.about.com
Award-winning books for children

www.cricketmag.com
Magazines for children from six months to six years

Lewis, Valerie and Mayes, Walter. *Valerie and Walter's Best Books for Children,* Quill, 2004.
Recommended books for children from birth through elementary school

Trelease, Jim. *The Read-Aloud Handbook,* Penguin Group, Sixth edition, 2006.
The importance of reading aloud to children

MUSIC

www.kididdles.com
Melodies and lyrics for more than 2,000 songs

www.kids.niehs.nih.gov/games/songs
Site includes music, games, puzzles and science activities

Rainville, Anna. *Singing Games, For Families, Schools and Communities,* Rudolf Steiner College Press, 2006.
Songs with simple melodies and movement instructions

OUTDOORS

Carson, Rachel. *The Sense of Wonder,* Harper Collins, text copyright, 1956, revised, 1998.
Encourages appreciation of nature by children and adults

www.lastchildinthewoods
Environmental awareness in children based on the book by Richard Louv

www.sharonlovejoy.com
Gardening with children

TOYS, GAMES AND COOKING

www.chinaberry.com
Toys, games and books listed by age

www.forsmallhands.com
Source for child-sized tools

www.familypastimes.com
Cooperative games for all ages beginning at age three

www.hearthsong.com
American-made toys, games and crafts for young children

Katzen, Mollie and Henderson, Ann. *Pretend Soup and Other Real Recipes,* Tricycle Press, 1994.
Appealing recipes with step-by-step illustrations for young cooks

www.magiccabin.com
Toys and fanciful dress-ups for preschoolers

INDEX

GRAMMIE NOTES